THE ENCYCLOPEDIA
OF PAPERMAKING
& BOOKBINDING

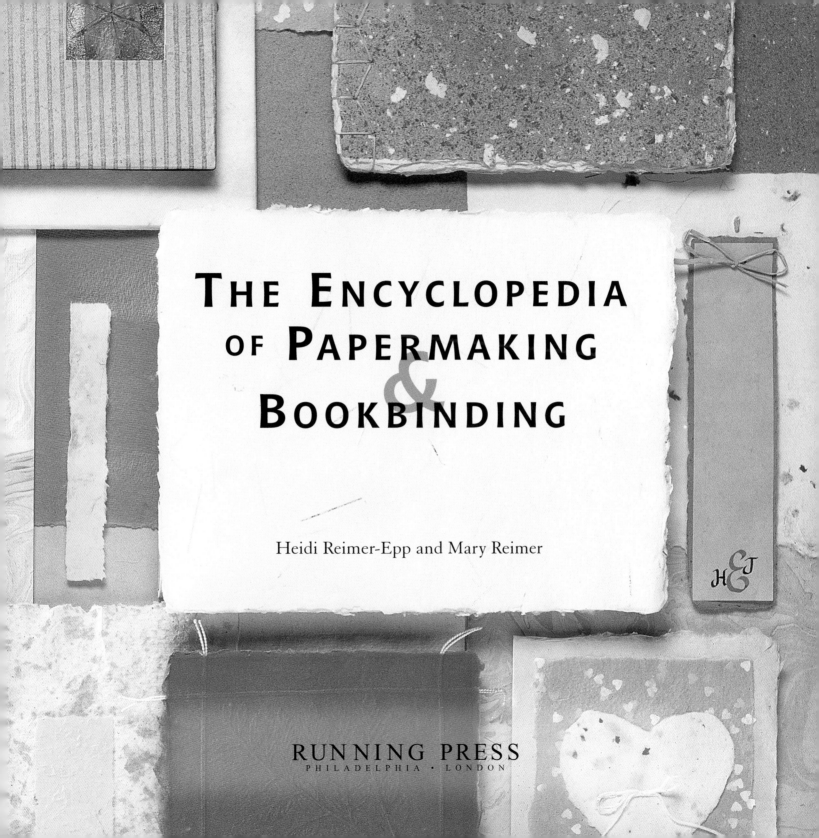

THE ENCYCLOPEDIA
OF PAPERMAKING
&
BOOKBINDING

Heidi Reimer-Epp and Mary Reimer

RUNNING PRESS
PHILADELPHIA · LONDON

A QUARTO BOOK

Library of Congress Cataloging-in-Publication Number 2001096256

ISBN 0-7624-1214-3

Conceived, designed, and produced by
Quarto Publishing plc
The Old Brewery
6 Blundell Street
London N7 9BH

QUAR.EPMT

Project editor Nadia Naqib
Senior art editor Sally Bond
Designer Heather Blagden
Copy editor Heather Haynes
Assistant art director Penny Cobb
Photographer Paul Forrester
Proofreader Sue Viccars
Picture researcher Sandra Assersohn
Indexer Pamela Ellis

Art director Moira Clinch
Publisher Piers Spence

Manufactured by Universal Graphics, Singapore
Printed by Leefung-Asco Printers Ltd, China

The authors and
publisher can accept
no liability for the use
or misuse of any
materials mentioned
in this book. Always
read all product
labels, and take all
necessary precautions.

This book may be ordered by mail from the publisher. Please include
$2.50 for postage and handling. But try your bookstore first!

Running Press Book Publishers
125 South Twenty-second Street
Philadelphia, Pennsylvania 19103-4399

Visit us on the web!
www.runningpress.com

Contents

INTRODUCTION

If you look around your home or office, you will probably be able to see paper in many different forms. Practical uses of paper in everyday life range from the wrapping around your latest purchase, paper toweling in the kitchen, wallpaper in the living room, newspaper on the front porch, the bedroom lampshade, the stuff in your fax machine and your laser printer, to the letter which comes by mail. Think about paper money, checks, artist's paper, paper plates and cups, paper for calligraphers, paper for packaging breakfast cereals and biscuits, and so much more! Paper has even been used in making chairs, shoes, and clothing. As a result, we struggle today to be careful consumers of our trees and other resources and to eliminate needless waste, to bridge the gap between convenience and our responsibility for a precious resource.

What exactly is paper and what is not? Dard Hunter, the father of the modern papermaking revival, has given the world this classic definition:

▲ Paper, in its many different forms and guises, makes up a vital part of our everyday lives.

To be classed as true paper the thin sheets must be made from fiber that has been macerated until each individual filament is a separate unit; the fibers intermixed with water, and by the use of a sieve-like screen, the fibers are lifted from the water in the form of a thin stratum, the water draining through the small openings of the screen, leaving a sheet of matted fiber upon the screen's surface. This thin layer of intertwined fiber is paper.

▲ Dard Hunter is widely credited for the modern renaissance in hand papermaking and printing.

▶ The short seed hairs of the cotton plant are one source of strong, durable paper.

Plant material such as leaves, wood, cotton, straw, hemp, grass, or flax can be broken down, chemically or mechanically, industrially or by hand, to reveal the natural cellulose contained within plant products. This material may be beaten, then dispersed in water from which can be made sheets of paper. The cellulose enables the bonding of the plant fibers, which expand in the water and are pulled closer together in the drying process.

Human beings share a common need for self-expression and communication that goes back to the first humans on earth.

▼ Different plant materials offer an endless variety of cellulose-based materials from which to make paper.

▲ Sumerian tablet account of donkeys harnessed for plowing, c.2360 BC.

Symbols painted on stone walls have endured through the ages and records of words chiseled in stone (Deuteronomy 10:1-2) remind us that we are part of a process that has developed over time. Stone tablets gave way to clay, metal, wax-covered wood, and, in time, to more convenient and cheaper alternatives. Books developed as a means of preserving written communication and so their history follows the development of civilization and the growing necessity of recording information. The ancient Sumerians are credited with having the first written language that used a system of wedge-shaped symbols or "cuneiform." The shapes were scratched onto clay tablets and sometimes preserved inside clay tubes.

The papyrus plant was used by the ancient Egyptians to form a writing surface by the same name. Papyrus was used as the primary writing material for about 4,000 years and the word "paper" is derived from this material. Papyrus is not, by definition, actually paper since it was made by placing strips of the plant stalk side by side with a second layer placed at right

documents. Today, machine-made vellums are much in demand. The Romans used a sharp wooden stylus to scratch letters into wax-covered wooden or metal tablets. Hinged books appeared which joined two or more tablets with leather hinges. Binding and embellishing the covers of these first books developed into an art form, with leather covering the boards and vellum or parchment for pages. The books were the possessions of the wealthy and scribes, and monks and slaves were involved in the process of creating and copying these works. Precious metals and jewels were used to enrich and enhance the covers and leathers were treated, dyed, tooled, and embossed with great care and pride. Girdle books, chained books, and the child's primer horn books may be found in collections today.

▲ Demonstration of how papyrus was prepared (above) before it was pounded to form the writing sheet shown left.

angles. The two sheets were then pounded together to form the writing surface. These sheets, which measured about 12 x 16 in (30 x 40 cm), were rolled onto sticks to form scrolls and were written on with reed pens. Later, other folded shapes were developed to contain important documents and records.

Animal skins were used to make parchment and vellum, which were, and still are, used for recording important

▶ A Franco-Flemish book 1475–80, showing the Coronation of the Virgin. One example of how animal skins were used to create parchment and vellum for books.

▲ This eighteenth-century sequence shows Japanese craftsmen making paper.

Various forms of leaves and bark were used as writing materials in India and Asia. In China, bamboo, silk, and wood were used but they provided writing surfaces that were too heavy, expensive, or cumbersome for extensive use. The development of paper as we know it took place over a period of more than 2,000 years. However, the invention of paper is credited to an official of the imperial court, by the name of T'sai Lun, who worked relentlessly to develop a writing surface suitable for the queen. Papermaking was a carefully kept secret for over 500 years, before it spread to Japan and Korea where it was used extensively in recording sacred texts and prayers. From there, it expanded to India by way of Chinese prisoners taken in battle and, eventually, to Morocco. Papermaking soon spread to Europe where cotton and linen rags provided the material for pulp.

With the development of the printing press in the fifteenth century came a need for cheaper, readily available material. Refined wood pulp was in common use by the end of the nineteenth century. The use of wood pulp in papermaking began early in the eighteenth century from the observations of a French naturalist. Réné de Réaumur noticed that the paperlike nests of wasps are formed from wood fibers which they chew into a powder and mix with an adhesive produced within the wasp, to become the tough water-resistant nest. One hundred years later, Charles Fenerty, a young Canadian, succeeded in making a machine to turn wood into pulp. Unfortunately, his years of work resulted in the production of only one sheet of paper!

The race was on to develop a machine to make paper from wood pulp and, in 1798, the Frenchman Nicholas-Louis Robert produced a crude machine which is the prototype of modern papermaking machines. Just a few years later, the English Fourdrinier brothers developed a new and improved version and the era of machine-made paper had begun.

Today, most of our paper is made from wood pulp, often cleaned and bleached and then sprayed onto moving mesh belts. The continuous sheet is

▲ The development of papermaking drew its inspiration from the natural world, when Réné de Réaumur examined the paperlike nests of wasps.

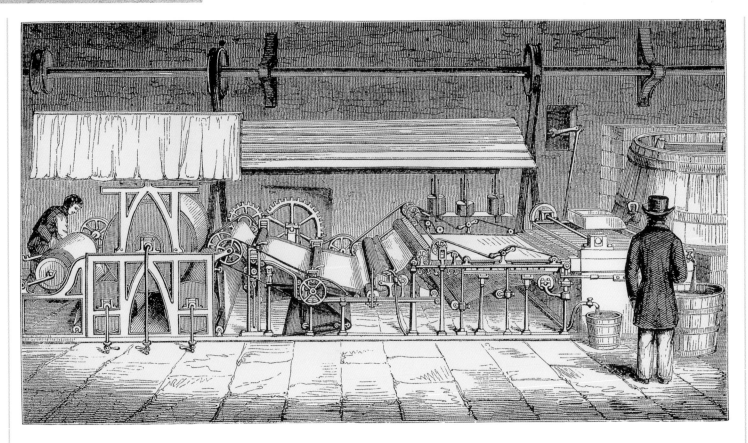

moved through a suction process, then heat-dried and wound onto huge reels. Many artists still prefer to use handmade paper because it can be durable, colorfast, and lightfast. It may be made to the specifications of the individual artist—rough or smooth, absorbent or impervious to water. In the west, cotton pulp is most commonly used for sheet formation, with abaca, flax, and hemp gaining popularity for the many variations possible. In the eastern method of sheet formation, paper is formed on a flexible screen, or *su*, made of bamboo. The screen fits into a hinged wooden frame or *geta*. The sheet is couched and the screen carefully peeled away to leave a thin layer of pulp. Repeated couchings are built up upon each other to form a sheet of great strength and beauty; this is then rolled onto a prepared board and air-dried.

Contemporary bookbinders use traditional and contemporary methods and materials to produce wonderful

▲ Example of the Fourdrinier papermaking machine, which was a development on the machine invented by Nicholas-Louis Robert.

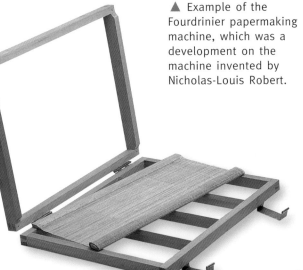

► The equipment for the eastern method of sheet forming consists of a ribbed mold, a flexible screen made of bamboo, or *su*, and a hinged wooden frame or *geta*.

examples of design and technique. The basic concept has not changed much since the first books were developed, but new technology and materials allow for creative freedom and diversity as never before. In this book, you can learn how to combine the skills and artistry of papermaking and bookbinding to join in the renewal of interest in this ancient art form.

◀ Modern-day artists demonstrate the remarkable forms paper can take. This scene by Gail Stiffe, entitled "Coorong—The Barrages" is made of recycled archival paper and dye.

▲ This highly complex modern-day papermaking machine is a far cry from the methods and machines of old.

◀ A different take on bookmaking. This work, by Philip Smith, entitled "Book in Sculptured Hands" was made with carved balsa-wood reinforced with epoxy putty and covered with goatskin.

CHAPTER 1

Papermaking Techniques and Projects

THIS SECTION IS MADE UP OF TWO PARTS, ONE EACH FOR PAPERMAKING TECHNIQUES AND PAPERMAKING PROJECTS. THE TECHNIQUES SECTION DESCRIBES THE BASIC AND MORE ADVANCED TECHNIQUES OF PAPERMAKING, FROM PULLING SHEETS TO LAMINATING AND EMBOSSING. THE PROJECTS BUILD ON THE TECHNIQUES LEARNED AND HAVE BEEN CHOSEN TO HELP YOU USE YOUR SKILLS AND TO MOVE ON IN YOUR PAPERMAKING EXPERIENCE. OF COURSE, RESULTS WILL VARY ACCORDING TO THE EQUIPMENT AVAILABLE AND EACH PERSON'S SKILL LEVEL, BUT USE THESE GENERAL GUIDELINES TO DISCOVER WHAT WORKS BEST FOR YOU. PRODUCE WORKS OF ART TO DECORATE YOUR HOME OR OFFICE, AND DELIGHT YOUR FRIENDS BY SENDING LETTERS AND GREETINGS ON YOUR PERSONAL STATIONERY AND GREETING CARDS. MORE IMPORTANTLY, USE THESE IDEAS AS A SPRINGBOARD FOR YOUR OWN CREATIVE PROJECTS. HAPPY PAPERMAKING!

BEFORE YOU START

Tools, Equipment, and Materials

One of the many wonderful features of making paper by hand is the ease with which you may begin. Equipment is readily available and easy to assemble. Cost is modest, depending upon the mold and deckle set used.

The tools and equipment described in this section will enable you to set up your hand papermill at home and to produce good quality sheets of paper, depending, of course, upon how much you practice! As you learn and develop as a papermaker, you will develop the set of tools which suits you best. If you are making your own molds, try a variety of screening materials to determine which produce the results you like. Most of all, enjoy the whole process of setting up and preparing your workplace. Prepare a journal to record your findings and methods and be sure to keep all tools and equipment scrupulously clean and dry when not in use. A sheet of plastic ceiling grid placed on the floor provides a good draining and drying surface on which to place damp molds and deckles, whisks, and blender parts at the end of a papermaking session.

TIP *Use rust-resistant staples or nails to attach the mesh to the frame. Then apply two layers of sealant to the edges.*

MOLD AND DECKLE

The molds and deckles used over the centuries by dedicated professional papermakers are masterful works of design and craftsmanship. The mold is simply a frame with mesh stretched over it to catch the pulp and allow the water to drain through. The deckle is a frame, not unlike the mold, but completely open with no mesh stretched across it. During papermaking, the deckle rests on top of the mesh side of the mold to confine the pulp to the size of the screened area, giving definition to the sheet of paper. This basic and essential piece of papermaking equipment may determine whether you enjoy the process of making a sheet of paper, or whether you experience frustration and defeat. Making a sheet is not difficult, but your mold and deckle will determine the success of your experience.

Expensive mold and deckle sets are available through papermaking suppliers and through auctions of secondhand equipment. Cheaper sets can be made from pieces of window screening edged with adhesive tape, or pieces of wire screening or fabric mesh can be stretched over a picture frame to make a mold. An identical frame without the screening may be used as the deckle. The purpose of the mold is to strain out water, leaving the fiber to form the sheet of paper. The sheet may be formed without using a deckle but the edges will be undefined and sloppy. The deckle gives shape to the sheet

TIP *When attaching a piece of screening to a frame, take great care to stretch the mesh tightly across the frame. Bulges in the mesh will cause uneven pockets of pulp and therefore uneven sheets of paper.*

of paper while allowing for the natural "deckle edge" to form on every side, which is a distinctive feature of handmade paper. Many attempts have been made to reproduce the deckle edge—even using a pair of scissors to "cut" a deckle edge into a plain sheet of paper!

The quality of your mold and deckle will affect the quality of your finished sheets. As you experiment and develop your skills and technique, you will probably want to invest in better quality equipment. For beginners, a 5½ x 8½ in (14 x 21 cm) sheet of paper is a convenient size for a regular kitchen basin. Remember that the final sheet will be the size of the inside measurement of your deckle.

Many commercially available molds are made using a heat-shrinking polypropylene mesh, which is remarkably strong and taut and can be tightened by using the heat of a hair dryer or hot water on the surface of the screen. So, whether you are independently wealthy or are on a tight budget, you can make paper with great success and delight!

VAT

This is a container for holding the mixture of water and pulp from which you will form sheets of paper. It must be able to accommodate the mold and deckle in the act of sheet formation. A regular kitchen basin is a good size for a 5½ x

8½ in (14 x 21 cm) mold and deckle set. Anything larger may be difficult to work with in a small vat. Inexpensive plastic laundry tubs with snap-on legs, a drain, and a plug make good vats for up to 11 x 17 in (28 x 42½ cm) sheets. Beyond that, an old bathtub mounted on a stand, or a specially constructed wooden box lined with plastic, are possibilities.

BLENDER

The method and length of beating time will determine the quality and appearance of your paper. The Hollander beater was developed by Peter Gentenaar in the late seventeenth century to produce pulp from cloth by beating or stamping the cloth until the fibers are broken down into a pulp. The Hollander can also be used to beat raw fibers, even long fibers such as flax. If you have access to a Hollander beater you are very fortunate. If not, you may purchase dry pulp from suppliers and reconstitute it in a home blender; these are readily available at garage sales and secondhand shops.

FELTS

This term refers to the fabric upon which each sheet of paper is "couched" or laid down. The felt, or surface fabric, helps to hold the edge of the newly formed sheet as it is rolled off the mold and onto the felt. It also helps to absorb the water from the new sheet, since the sheet at this stage is said to be 96 percent water. As the sheets are pressed, the felt absorbs and pulls away the water as the fibers of pulp lock together to form a strong bond. Authentic felting material is expensive and difficult to acquire. For our purpose, there are many options. We recommend using old wool blankets (often available from thrift stores) which have been washed and put in a hot dryer to shrink and mat. Cut the blankets into rectangles 3–4 in (7½–10 cm) larger than your sheets and you are ready to begin. You may also use toweling or sheeting, but remember that the need for absorbency will affect drying time and paper strength.

The surface of your felting material will imprint on the sheet of paper. Use mesh dishcloths between each newly formed sheet. Experiment with a variety of surfaces to find what works best for you.

WIRE WHISK
You will need this to help in the even dispersement of pulp fibers within the vat of water. If working with more than one pulp type at a time, use two whisks or carefully wash the whisk each time you change vats.

SPONGE
This may help to absorb water in the sheet during the couching process and can help to release the sheet from the mold.

PULP
The three materials most commonly used for pulp by papermakers in home-based papermills are cotton, abaca, and recycled paper. Recycled papers are readily available in every home and office. Recycled office paper, advertisements, tissue paper, paper toweling, and wrapping paper are all usable in forming new sheets. A word of caution on using recycled material: additives and chemicals are added to most commercially made papers, and your final product will contain these impurities, which will affect its quality and durability.

Many different plant, animal, and synthetic products can provide fiber for papermaking. Semiprocessed pulp, such as 100 percent cotton, and abaca, a product of the banana leaf, are available through papermaking suppliers; these pulp bases will result in high quality sheets of paper. Hemp and flax are interesting fibers to use. Each pulp dries at a different rate so be sure to experiment with several kinds. Combine semiprocessed pulps in equal parts with recycled pulp, to improve the strength and durability of the papers and allow you to use up some of the paper which might otherwise be thrown into landfills. Experiment to find materials, methods, combinations, and recipes, which please you. Pulp made from vegetables requires some special handling and this will be discussed in more detail in the Advanced Techniques section (see page 44).

Setting Up

Now that you have assembled your
equipment, you are ready to set up
your hand papermill. To do so you
will need to establish two areas:
one for setting up the vat and
another place beside the vat on which
to place the pulp that you have
scooped. You will also need a third area
for pressing and a fourth area for drying,
which we will address later (see Pressing, page
29, and Drying, page 30).

PREPARING A COUCHING PAD

Begin by placing a pad of
folded newspapers under
one of your felt pieces. This
will give a bulge to your
couching pad and make it
easier to roll the mold over
the surface to break the
surface tension between the
fibers and the mold. Place
a mesh dishcloth over the
blanket or felt, dampen the
entire surface area, and you
are ready to couch your
first sheet (see Couching,
page 26).

PREPARING THE VAT

Half-fill your basin with
water. Do not use ice-cold
water as your hands are
going to be spending a
lot of time in there, but
remember that warm water
will deteriorate the pulp
quicker than cool water!
Add about a cup of pulp
and whisk vigorously to
disperse the fibers evenly
in the water. The amount of
pulp will vary and you
will develop a feel for the
thickness of each sheet
as you work. Add pulp as
necessary, but whisk after
each addition.

Pulp Preparation

Careful preparation of pulp will help to make your papermaking experience a success. Choose the type of pulp you will be using and prepare it according to the following directions.

Always work with small amounts in your blender, blend thoroughly to avoid clumps and specks in your paper, and store unused pulp in a refrigerator. Alternatively, you may squeeze out any excess water from the pulp and store the balls of pulp in the freezer or dehydrate them by airdrying and storing them in a dry place. Reused pulp may be of a slightly lower quality than newly prepared pulp but it is great for paper casting, layering, and blending.

In this section, we will demonstrate how to process cotton, abaca, and recycled paper into pulp using a kitchen blender and other easily available equipment.

YOU WILL NEED
- **semiprocessed cotton pulp**
- **bowl of water**
- **kitchen blender**
- **abaca**
- **scissors**
- **shredded office paper, wrapping paper, or magazines**
- **bowl or bucket**
- **strainer**
- **jar of water**

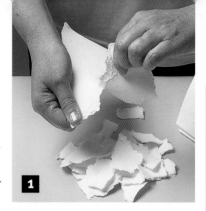

1 Tear semiprocessed cotton pulp into 1 in (2½ cm) pieces to prepare for the blender. Soak the pieces in a bowl of water for at least half an hour before adding about five or six at a time to a blender.

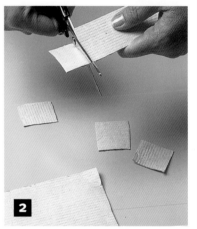

2 Abaca is a tougher fiber than semi-processed cotton. Cut the semiprocessed pulp with scissors into 1 in (2½ cm) pieces. It breaks down quickly in water but it is a good idea to soak it for at least half an hour before blending. Add about four or five pieces at a time to a blender three-quarters-full of water.

3 Tear shredded office paper, wrapping paper, or pages from magazines into 2 in (5 cm) pieces. Longer strips will wrap around the shaft of a blender mechanism and strangle it. Bear in mind that the quality of what goes into the blender will determine the quality of the final product.

4 It is always best to soak pulp in water for at least half an hour, but overnight is even better. This begins the process of breaking down the fibers and making the pulp easier to beat, and is also kind to your blender as it will not have to work so hard!

7 To check if your pulp is ready for the vat, take a pinch of well-beaten pulp and drop it into a jar of water.

5 Once you have added the pieces of soaked semi-processed cotton, abaca, or shredded office paper to the blender, secure the lid tightly in place before starting the motor. Blend in short bursts, checking frequently to make sure the pulp has not collected around the blade. When there appears to be an even consistency of fibers in the water, with no obvious lumps, do the jar test (see step 7) to determine whether the pulp is ready for the vat.

8 Screw the lid on tightly, then shake the jar vigorously for one minute.

9 Hold the jar up to the light and examine the pulp for even consistency. If clumps of fiber are visible, more blending is required.

6 Strain the pulp and store it in a bowl or bucket until you have blended the amount you want, adding each strained blender load to the bowl.

TIP *Avoid using newspaper to make pulp as it will form a gray sludge in the vat and the final product is a weak and rather unattractive sheet.*

BASIC TECHNIQUES
Pulp Pigmentation

There are many ways in which to incorporate color into pulp. We will examine a few of the most accessible methods but feel free to experiment with your own ideas for color.

Plant dyes and natural pigments are a whole world waiting to be explored. Use the materials that work best for you in your situation. Specially designed papermaking pigments are available from suppliers and these will produce the most reliable results as well as being colorfast and lightfast. Other sources will be inferior to these pigments but, they are good sources of color for your paper adventures. As you discover the joy of papermaking, you will probably want to purchase these pigments in order to ensure a long-lasting, high-quality product. It is a good idea to write down in your papermaking journal the ingredients used for each type of paper you make, so that you can reproduce the great results. You never know when you will come up with a product that you or someone else wants to duplicate!

YOU WILL NEED
- papermaking pigment
- jars of water
- spoon
- blender containing beaten pulp
- powdered fabric dye
- colored paper napkins or construction paper
- colored tissue paper
- luster pigment
- petal or metallic confetti

PAPERMAKING PIGMENTS

1 Add a small amount of pigment to a jar of water. Remember that a little goes a long way.

2 Stir the diluted pigment well for about five minutes. This will make the distribution of the pigment within the pulp fibers more even.

3 Add the diluted pigment slowly to the beaten pulp in a blender. Mix the pulp and pigment well on a low speed.

FABRIC DYE

1 Dissolve powdered fabric dye according to the manufacturer's instructions.

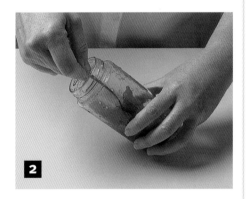

2 Mix well before adding it to the pulp. Make sure all the dye particles are dissolved before coming into contact with the pulp fibers.

4 For best absorption of the pigment, leave the pigmented pulp overnight before using. Then blend it once more before adding it to the vat. Check to see that the pigment has been absorbed by looking at the water surrounding the pigmented fiber. Is it clear or still holding some of the pigment? The clearer the water, the better the fibers have picked up all the particles of pigment.

TIP *Using retention agent to increase the absorption of the pigment by the fiber makes the best use of your time and energy and assures that you will achieve great results in your pigmenting ventures. This product is available from papermaking supply companies.*

COLORED PAPER

1 Tear colored paper napkins or construction paper into small pieces, approximately 1 in (2½ cm) square.

2 Add the wet paper squares to the beaten pulp in the blender.

3 Blend for about 10 seconds or until the colored paper is evenly mixed into the pulp.

TISSUE PAPER

1 Tear pieces of colored tissue paper into 1 in (2½ cm) squares. Use two or more colors at a time for a mottled effect.

TIP *Be sure to examine the blade of the blender to make sure that the paper is not wrapping around the blade. If this occurs, pull it off and tear it into smaller pieces. Blend again.*

2 Add the pieces to the prepared pulp and blend for a few seconds for a chunky pulp, or longer for a smooth pulp.

TIP *Sizing is used to seal the pulp after all the other steps have taken place. The sizing is like the period at the end of a sentence — it completes the task of pulp preparation and adds a water resistance to the paper to allow printing, calligraphy, watercolor, or whatever use you might have for your paper. The amount of sizing used will vary according to the purpose for the paper. Always dilute the sizing in water before adding it to the pulp. Mix it in thoroughly and, for best results, allow the pulp to rest overnight before using.*

SPARKLE PIGMENT

1 Add a lustrous sheen to pigmented or plain paper sheets by adding luster pigment to the pulp. This is a special pigment containing tiny particles of mica and other minerals which are held by the fibers in the pulp following the addition of retention agent, as discussed on page 21. Available at papermaking suppliers, this is for those occasions when you really want to try something unique. Dissolve the luster pigment well in a jar of water.

2 Add the diluted luster pigment to the prepared pulp and blend well.

INCLUSIONS

1 Handmade papers with petal or metallic confetti inclusions are among the most popular paper types for stationery, invitations, and gift products. There are a few things to consider before adding these inclusions to your pulp to avoid disappointment. The best time to add most inclusions is during beating. Process them for only a few seconds but long enough to incorporate them into the pulp.

2 Stirring inclusions or mixing them by hand into the beaten pulp is satisfactory, but will result in more flaking than the blended version. Alternatively, you could try sprinkling the petals on top of the pulled sheet. This looks nice and allows you to control where the petals are placed but, sadly, most of these petals will fall off once the paper is dry. They may be reattached with a spot of glue if the effect is worth the effort.

TIP *Not all petals or petal combinations can be used successfully. Deep red and burgundy petals bleed a blue color into the surrounding pulp. White petals tend to turn brown. Any tiny bit of green can tint a whole vat yellow, so pick through your petals carefully to remove anything green. Using plants and petals as sources of color is a whole area worthy of exploration for the papermaker. Marigold petals will produce a natural dye, as will tea and coffee, for example. Be sure to record your recipes and results.*

Pulling a Sheet

Once the vat is set up, a couching pad prepared, and the pulp ready, you may begin to pull sheets of paper from the vat.

The first sheet is often like the first pancake in a stack—it is the most difficult to make. It may stick to the mold, or be too thick or too thin, or full of holes. With each piece you pull it will become easier, so get started and do not worry if things go wrong. Build a stack of sheets, keep notes on the process, and then observe the finished sheets. You may be surprised that some of your doubtful pieces turn out to be the most interesting ones!

YOU WILL NEED
- vat for preparing pulp
- paper pulp
- cup
- wire whisk
- mold and deckle
- duct tape
- kitchen spatter screen

1 Fill the vat half-full with water. Add one cup of pulp to the vat.

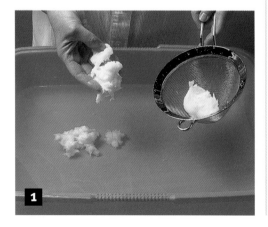

2 Using a wire whisk, mix the water and pulp thoroughly until they form an even mixture.

3 Add more pulp as necessary to make sheets of paper with the thickness you desire. Whisk well after each addition of pulp.

4 Wet the surface of the mold's screen by laying it on the water. Remember that the sheet is formed on top of the mold.

5 Holding the deckle on top of the mold with thumbs on top, reach toward the back of the vat and, in one continuous motion, pull the mold and deckle under the surface and up again.

6 As you begin to pull upward, hold the mold and deckle level with the surface of the water. This will make the pulp disperse evenly on the screen. Tipping the mold will cause thick deposits of pulp in some places and, as a result, a poor-quality sheet of paper.

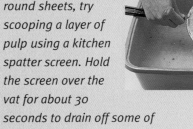

TIP *For making round sheets, try scooping a layer of pulp using a kitchen spatter screen. Hold the screen over the vat for about 30 seconds to drain off some of the water before couching.*

7 Lift the mold and deckle straight up and out of the vat, breaking the surface tension and allowing some of the water to drain.

9 To return a ruined sheet to the vat, hold the mold, pulp facing downward. With a quick, firm motion, touch the mold's face to the surface of the water in the vat.

10 The pulp lifts off and may be whisked into the vat and reused. This is called "kissing off!"

8 Carefully remove the deckle from the mold to avoid dropping excess water—called "vatman's tears"—on the freshly formed sheet. If this or any other flaw appears at this stage, it is easy to return the pulp to the vat and try again (see steps 9 and 10).

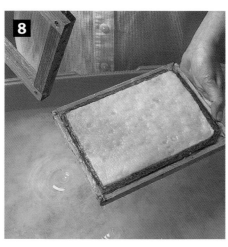

11 Use duct tape to mask off a smaller sized mold for your sheet pulling. Wipe any excess pulp off the edges before couching your freshly made sheet of paper.

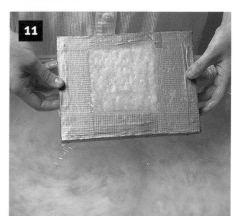

Couching

The process of transferring the newly formed sheet onto another surface is called "couching." The term comes from the French verb *coucher* meaning to lay down, a precise description of this technique, which allows multiple sheetforming with a single mold. The sheets are stacked in a "post" which can be up to 30 sheets high.

YOU WILL NEED
- newspapers
- two waterproofed boards
- blankets or towels
- mesh dishcloths
- mold and deckle
- sponge
- heavy felt

1 Place a pad of folded newspaper, or a folded piece of blanket, on a board which has been treated with a waterproof coating. This makes it easier to roll the mold and deckle onto the couching surface, establishing connection between the pulp sheet and the surface of the couching pad.

2 Cover the pad with a blanket or piece of towel to make an absorbent layer.

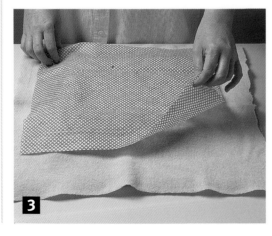

3 Lay a mesh kitchen cloth on top and smooth out any wrinkles which may affect the paper.

4 Pour water over the entire couching pad to increase the connection between the pulp and couching surface. The pad should be damp rather than soaking wet.

5 Resting the edge of the mold on the cloth edge nearest you, begin to roll the mold onto the cloth in a continuous motion.

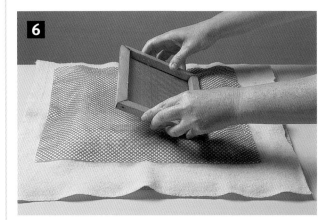

6 Continue this motion until the mold lies flat on the couching pad.

7 Press down firmly on the edges of the mold to make contact with the cloth.

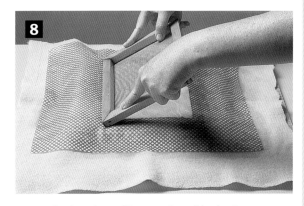

8 Continuing the rolling motion, lift the bottom edge, and roll the mold off the pad.

TIP *If the sheet does not release, use a sponge to blot away some of the water. Then repeat the rolling action.*

9 This leaves the newly formed sheet behind on the couching pad.

10 If the sheet tears or folds, simply roll the pulp off the cloth or "kiss it off" on the water's surface and reuse it in the vat, being sure to whisk it again first.

11 Cover the sheet with two mesh dishcloths and repeat the process of forming a sheet on top of the cloth. Cover with two more cloths until you form a stack of newly formed paper sheets and separating cloths.

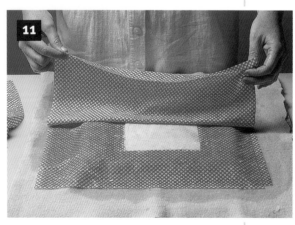

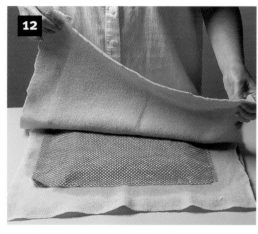

12 Cover the stack or post with a piece of heavy felt or blanket.

13 Place a waterproofed board on top of the stack and prepare to press.

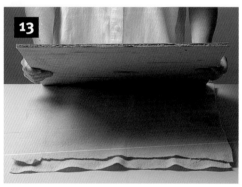

▼ A pair of waterproofed boards and four G-clamps (below) can be used to remove water from freshly made paper (see opposite).

Pressing

Since the sheets you have just formed consist of about 96 percent water, you must find a way to remove some of that water quickly to allow the sheet to begin to dry.

The best way to do this is to construct a press to squeeze the water out and to maintain firm, even pressure so that the fibers will bond to make a strong piece of paper. Here are some ways of doing this, but make sure that you are prepared for the gush of water which will initially spill out of the press. A tray or mat with a lip around the edge to catch drops of water may work for a small press. Working outdoors solves the problem of overflow but is not always feasible. Experiment with what works in your situation.

YOU WILL NEED
- stack of newly formed sheets
- four G-clamps or several heavy bricks
- tray or mat

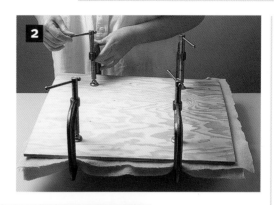

2 Tighten each clamp until water stops pouring from the stack.

3 If G-clamps are unavailable, use something heavy, such as a pile of heavy bricks, to apply weight to the stack.

4 After pressing, the damp sheets should be strong enough to pick up and place on the drying system.

1 Using the two water-proofed boards as the press, attach four G-clamps evenly around the boards to hold the press in place.

◀ A specialist screw press is ideal for expelling water from a post of freshly made sheets.

Drying

As in all aspects of papermaking, each papermaker will develop methods that best suit the particular surroundings, available materials, and varying conditions of his or her location.

YOU WILL NEED
- clothesline or clothes rack
- wooden clothespins
- couched sheet
- iron
- brayer (small roller)
- glass or linoleum
- knife
- plywood
- corrugated cardboard sheets
- sheets of cotton linter pulp
- bricks or tension straps
- fan

Temperature, humidity, space, the availability of a power source, and time are all factors in determining which drying method to use. We will look at several. Try each one and invent others as you experiment to find your best way of working.

HANGING THE SHEET TO DRY

This simple method of drying sheets requires a clothesline or clothes rack, some wooden clothespins, and a couched sheet on its mesh dishcloth backing. Overlap the edge of the backing cloth and secure to the line using two clothespins. When dry, carefully peel the paper sheet from the backing. Press with a warm iron to flatten completely. If extra sizing is required, use a spray sizing while pressing.

ROLLING ONTO A SMOOTH SURFACE

1 Use a small brayer or roller to roll the pressed sheet carefully onto a smooth surface, such as glass, linoleum, or an untextured counter top. The side against the surface will be smooth and glossy while the airdried surface will be rougher.

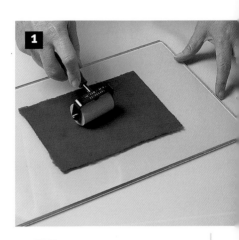

2 When the sheet has dried, use a knife to loosen the edges.

3 Carefully peel the sheet off the glass.

SETTING UP A DRYER SYSTEM

1 This is the best way to deal with several sheets of paper in a small space. Begin with two pieces of plywood, each one 2 x 2 ft (60 x 60 cm) for a small system. Coat all surfaces of the plywood with a waterproofing treatment. Several coats will extend the system's life and effectiveness.

2 Start to build a sandwich, beginning with the plywood. Add a layer of corrugated cardboard.

3 Then add a layer of cotton linter pulp in sheet form.

4 Lay a sheet of pressed, newly-formed paper. Repeat the "filling" to accommodate all your paper to a maximum of about 2 ft (60 cm), and then top with the second piece of plywood. Weigh the stack down with bricks or strap it tightly with tension straps. Set a fan to blow at one end of the sandwich. This will set up a current of air, pulling the damp air out of the stack and bringing dry air through the other side. This size makes a portable drying system, which is easily dismantled for storage or change of location.

ADVANCED TECHINQUES
Laminating

One of the most versatile and interesting techniques in papermaking is laminating. This involves couching two or more sheets on top of each other which bond together during pressing and drying to form a single, solid sheet of paper.

YOU WILL NEED
- vat of prepared pulp
- mold and deckle
- flowers, leaves, feathers, or other small objects
- thread for guidelines
- wool
- vat of contrasting colored pulp

With this technique, the possibilities for creative papermakers are endless, so it is well worth the effort to learn. The skill lies in lining up the thin sheets of pulp so that they are placed exactly where you want them to be, whether directly on top of the base sheet, or at angles, or randomly applied. The choice is yours.

LAMINATING SMALL OBJECTS

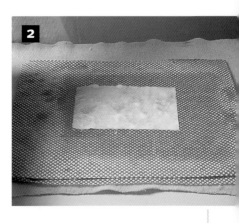

1 Pull a sheet from the vat in the usual way.

2 Couch this sheet, creating a base sheet upon which to couch a second.

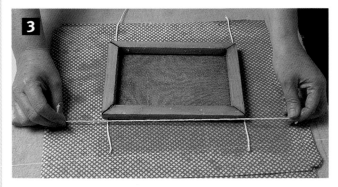

3 To couch the second sheet precisely on top of the first, lightly position the deckle on the couched sheet and mark the outside edges with thread.

4 Remove the deckle. At this stage you may place flowers, leaves, or any other small object that you wish to laminate on top of the sheet.

5 Now pull and couch a second sheet directly on top of the first sheet, using the threads as guidelines.

6 Carefully lift the mold and deckle away. Press in a single layer to avoid embossing the feather in other sheets of paper as it is pressed.

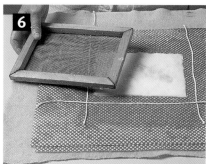

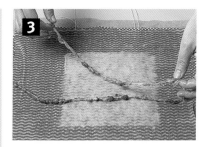

3 Add more lengths of dipped wool to the sheet, overlapping them as desired.

4 Cover this base sheet with a second sheet couched directly on top of the first.

5 Press and dry these sheets separately to avoid embossing the threads onto other sheets.

LAMINATING WOOL

1 Try laminating two sheets with wool between them. Begin by dipping lengths of wool into a contrasting colored pulp.

6 When dry, pull the ends of the wool to create textural surprises.

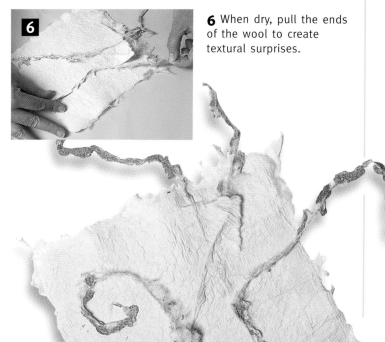

2 Place the wool carefully across a newly formed sheet.

Working with Texture

One of the wonderful qualities of handmade paper is that it takes on the texture of the material upon which it is couched.

YOU WILL NEED
- patterned towel
- mold and deckle
- vat of prepared pulp
- sponge
- synthetic netting
- bubble wrap
- textured glass
- brayer (small roller)
- knife
- plastic bag

This provides the creative papermaker with the challenge of exploring various couching surfaces and materials, and of studying and recording the results in a journal. Staple or insert a small sample of your textured paper along with an explanation of how you achieved that result. Keep in mind that some surfaces present challenges in the couching process.

PATTERNED TOWEL

1 This waffle-patterned towel should make an interesting surface on which to couch a sheet.

2 When the surface material is rough or fuzzy, it is difficult to achieve surface attraction and you may need to sponge the mold, pour a little water over it, or flick the mold along the edge with your fingernail, to release the sheet.

SYNTHETIC NETTING

1 A piece of synthetic netting makes a great textural pattern upon which to couch a sheet of cotton.

2 Couch the sheet over the netting. Press separately and hang to dry, or dry under a weight.

BUBBLE WRAP

1 Bubble wrap provides an interesting textural surface.

2 Use a brayer or roller to fix the sheet firmly to the glass surface, pressing into the pattern.

2 Carefully remove the mold, leaving the sheet to dry in place. Peel off when dry.

3 After the sheet has dried on the glass, loosen the edges with a knife.

TEXTURED GLASS

1 Here a sheet of damp, pressed paper is placed on a pane of textured glass.

4 The result is a beautifully textured sheet of paper.

JAPANESE MOMOGAMI

1 To make an easy form of the intricate Japanese Momogami paper, scrunch a sheet of damp, pressed paper into a tiny ball.

4 Open out the paper flat to reveal a beautifully textured sheet. This paper could be used in a Fold and Dip project (see page 48).

2 Tie it tightly into the corner of a plastic bag and leave overnight.

3 Remove the scrunched ball from the bag when completely dry.

Embossing

Embossing a piece of paper involves making an impression on the surface of the paper by exerting pressure on an object either under or on top of the sheet. For the greatest effect, use newly formed sheets that have been pressed but not dried. Allow the sheet to dry under pressure to form a sharp definition in the paper.

Look for objects and surfaces that can be used to emboss your paper. Some, like wire screening or mesh ribbon, are placed on the couching surface first. Then the damp sheet is placed on top with a protective cloth on top of that. Finally, bricks or a heavy board are placed on top and the sheet is allowed to air-dry. With other objects, such as the child's building panel used here, the paper is placed down first and the object is placed on top of the paper before being weighted down and allowed to dry.

YOU WILL NEED
- wire shape
- mold and deckle
- vat of prepared pulp
- child's building panel
- bricks or heavy board

PRESSURE FROM BELOW

1 Place a wire shape on the couching surface.

2 Couch a sheet of cotton on top so that the wire shape is positioned in the corner.

3 The sheet is now ready to be covered and weighted down.

PRESSURE FROM ABOVE

1 Here the sheet is placed on the couching surface before the shape is pressed down upon it.

2 Place the shape, here a child's building panel, on top, then cover the sheet and weight it to air-dry.

Layering

Layering uses the technique of laminating to combine a variety of pulp types and colors to create scenes and collages, and to reveal hidden colors within the single sheet of paper.

As with laminating, the damp layers of the newly formed sheets will become one as the fibers bond during pressing and drying. With this technique you are free to experiment. Try free-form layering, scooping away bits of pulp to reveal the colors beneath. Try precision layering where you work to achieve a particular result. Combine layering with embossing, adding threads to pull away outer layers and to add textural interest. Again, be sure to make notes in your journal as you work—you are bound to get carried away with this technique and, unless you write down what you are doing, you will not remember it later! If pen and paper keep getting wet as you try to record your work, put a chalkboard on the wall and later you may add the notes to your journal. Here are three layering techniques to get you started.

YOU WILL NEED
- **three colors of prepared pulp**
- **mold and deckle**
- **threads**

SCOOPING AWAY

1 Begin by putting some bits of colored pulp down onto the couching surface.

2 Next, couch a sheet of another color on top of the yellow bits.

3 Scoop away some of the white pulp with a fingernail, revealing some of the yellow beneath.

4 Couch a third color sheet over the white.

5 Press and dry the layered sheet.

SEE-THROUGH LAYERING

1 After couching a base sheet of white, take the mold and scoop a thin layer of contrasting pulp onto one end.

2 Line up the edges and laminate it onto the base sheet.

3 Pull a third layer of another color and couch it over the first two layers. The thinness of the layers allows the light to shine through, revealing the colors within.

LAYERING WITH THREADS

1 Prepare the base and the second layer as for "See-Through Layering," then lay a thread across the sheet.

2 Couch the third layer over the first two layers and the thread.

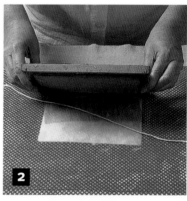

3 Pull the threads while the pulp is still damp. Then press and dry. Alternatively, wait until the sheet is dry before pulling the threads. When damp, the pulp peels off in a wider band, revealing more color from the layer beneath.

Paper Marbling

In the world of paper and paper arts, marbling, or the Japanese *suminagashi*, is without doubt the most delightful and enchanting technique. In its simplest form, anyone may achieve successful results. At its most highly developed form, the secrets of the art are not even divulged.

Based on the principle that oil and water do not mix, marbling involves floating an oil-based substance in several colors on the surface of water. The colors can be manipulated into patterns or left to form random swirls. A sheet of paper is placed on the surface and carefully peeled off, revealing the pattern of colors. Many wonderful books have been written on paper marbling for those who wish to delve into the craft more deeply. Here is a beginner's guide to get you started.

YOU WILL NEED

- shallow pan or wash basin
- prepared marbling inks, or oil paints and mineral spirits
- toothpicks or sharp stick
- toothbrush
- sheets of abaca paper, smaller than the pan being used
- pad of newspapers

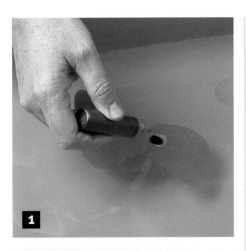

1 Fill the pan with 2–3 in (5–7 cm) of water. Apply a dot of marbling ink to the water. Some marbling kits contain a small blotting paper dot for dispersing the inks.

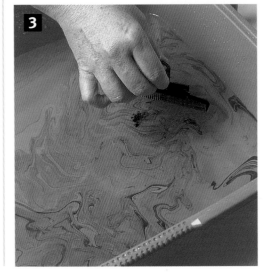

2 Apply a drop of each color to the first dot and watch as the colors spread across the surface. If using oil paints thinned with mineral spirits, use a toothbrush to spatter color across the water's surface.

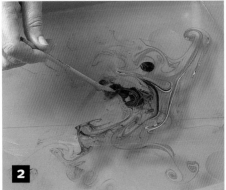

3 Using a toothpick or sharp stick, gently pull the colors. Here, a fine-tooth comb attached to a clip is used to pull the colors a little more. Avoid stirring the ink as this will blend all the colors into a rather muddy sameness.

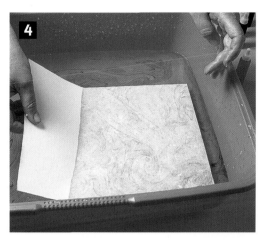

4 Gently lower the sheet of abaca paper onto the surface of the water.

6 Lift the sheet out of the pan by the corners in one smooth motion and place it to dry, pattern side up, on a pad of newspapers.

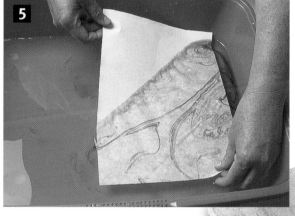

5 If you hold the sheet of abaca paper at diagonally opposite corners when lowering it into the water, you will allow yourself a little more control. Allow the paper to "roll" gently onto the water.

Paper Casting

So far in this book, we have dealt with paper as a two-dimensional form. Artists and sculptors have long worked with paper as a casting medium and most of us have experienced the delight of molding strips of papier-mâché around a form to make a mask or a pinata. Recently, paper casting has been reinvented as a craft for all those interested in working with paper and pulp.

Many detailed and beautiful molds are available commercially, although it is worth the effort to make your own molds and to use objects such as plastic packaging and jelly molds to make some original pieces. But, for home use and for basic mastery of the skill of paper casting, acquire a clay mold, cookie cutters, or candy-making molds, prepare some cotton pulp (see page 18), and get started. Cotton pulp is recommended because of its short fibers which make for low shrinkage and an ability to reproduce fine detail in the molds.

Pigment may be added according to the instructions given on pages 20–21. Many sources recommend using a release agent such as petroleum jelly or cooking spray.

YOU WILL NEED
- clay mold
- prepared cotton pulp
- sizing
- mesh dishcloth
- microwave and protective holders or oven mitts
- knife
- candy molds

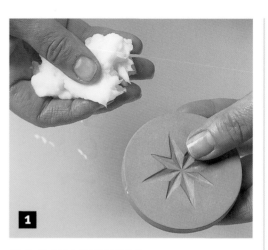

1 All you need for paper casting is a mold and some prepared cotton pulp with sizing. The sizing will make it easier to paint or embellish the finished piece.

2 Using small amounts of pulp at a time, push the pulp into all the crevices of the mold to reproduce every detail.

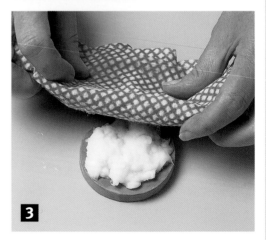

3 With a dry cloth, apply pressure to the pulp in the filled mold to bond the fibers of the cotton and to ensure that the pulp has been completely packed into the mold.

4 Continue to blot and press the pulp until water no longer comes out of it.

5 Allow the cast to air-dry in the mold or put it in a microwave oven for 30-second intervals. Depending on the microwave, this may take four or five repeats. Press down with a cloth in between times. The clay mold will be very hot so use protective holders or oven mitts when handling! When the cast is completely dry, use a knife to loosen the edges of the pulp.

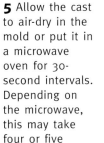

6 The finished product will be an exact duplicate of the inside surface of the mold. Now the cast is ready to be used as a decoration, an embellishment on a card, or as a gift item in itself.

USING OTHER MOLDS

1 Molds are available with four or more images on a related theme. Fill just one, two, or all four with pulp, if desired.

CANDY MOLDS

1 Candy-making molds may also be used. These are great for using up small amounts of leftover pulp.

2 Make several casts in a variety of shapes and colors and store in a dry place for future use.

Working with Fruit and Vegetable Pulp

Working with fruit and vegetable pulp requires special handling. There is no limit to the number of plants that may be used to produce pulp for the papermaker. Just look around you and you will see common weeds, flowers, and grains which, when properly processed, will result in some of the most exciting papers you have ever seen! Learn these basic techniques and then don't be afraid to try your own ideas. Just remember to keep notes in your journal and keep samples with each new recipe.

YOU WILL NEED
- carrot tops
- chopping board
- kitchen knife
- large pot
- strainer
- iris leaves
- fork
- fireplace ashes
- wooden spoon
- jug
- kitchen blender
- vat of water
- vat of prepared pulp
- bucket
- mold and deckle
- blankets and mesh dishcloths

PULP PREPARATION
To turn plant material into pulp, it is necessary to break it down to separate the fiber and to get rid of unwanted components in the plant. Some plants will only require cooking, while others will need a caustic solution to help the process. Here we show how to prepare pulp using carrot tops, which require cooking only, and then we demonstrate how to prepare pulp using fibrous iris leaves and a solution of water and fireplace ashes.

MAKING CARROT TOP PULP

1 Gather a mound of carrot tops, soak them overnight in water if time allows, then chop them into pieces no longer than 1 in (2½ cm).

2 Put the carrot tops into a pot with enough water to cover. Bring to a boil, then simmer for one to two hours, until the toughest bits pull apart easily.

3 Strain and rinse the plant material. Then place it in a blender before blending it to form sheets of paper (see Sheet Formation on page 46).

TIP *When working with vegetable and fruit pulp, it is even more important to keep all tools and equipment scrupulously clean to avoid contamination of other papers and to prevent nasty rotting of pulp.*

MAKING IRIS LEAF PULP

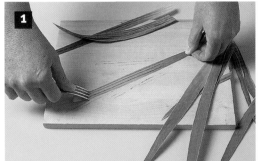

1 Scrape both sides of the iris leaves with the tines of a fork to help in the breaking down process.

2 Cut the leaves into 1–2 in (2½–5 cm) pieces.

3 Soak the pieces overnight in a pot full of water. This will begin the process of breaking down the plant material.

4 Prepare the alkaline solution by filling a pot half-full of fireplace ashes and covering with water.

5 Bring to a boil, stirring to dissolve most of the ash. Then strain the contents, discarding the undissolved product and saving the liquid solution.

6 Pour the liquid solution over the plant material to cover. Bring to a boil and simmer until the plant material is mushy and pulls apart easily. Strain and rinse the plant material several times to remove the alkaline solution.

SHEET FORMATION

Working with 100 percent plant material is challenging and requires care and patience. Try mixing equal parts of plant material and cotton pulp or abaca pulp for an interesting product which is stronger and easier to handle. But do try some pieces of 100 percent plant material. They are well worth the effort!

1 Blend handfuls of plant pulp in a blender two-thirds full of water. Use to form a small sheet, or drain and collect in a bucket until you have a larger amount.

2 It is only necessary to blend the plant material for a few seconds, depending on the coarseness of the paper desired. If a smoother paper is required, blend the material for a longer period of time.

3 Add the pulp to a vat of water and mix thoroughly.

4 Pull a sheet in the usual way, even though the pulp may seem uneven. Patch obvious holes by applying pulp to empty areas.

6 You may have to try several tricks to loosen the sheet as some pulp may stick to the mold (see TIP on page 27).

5 Couch the sheet in a rolling motion as for any pulp.

Fold and Dip

This variation on the tie-dye theme of the 1960s uses paper instead of fabric and bears some resemblance to the Japanese art of *shibori-zome* which combines intricate knot-tying with dyeing to create beautiful patterns.

YOU WILL NEED
- **sheet of abaca**
- **water spray**
- **bone folder or spoon handle**
- **clamp**
- **two colors of ink**

This simplified version uses a sheet of abaca, which is strong enough to withstand all the handling necessary. For greater effect, use a sheet that has been scrunched and dried (see page 36).

2 Start to fold the sheet of damp abaca into a fan.

3 Use a bone folder to crease the edges. If a bone folder is unavailable, use a spoon handle or other strong but blunt edge that will crease, but not tear, the paper.

1 Begin with a damp sheet for sharp creases and better spreading of the dye. Spray water over a dry sheet to dampen it.

4 Make folds about ¾ in (2 cm) wide. You can experiment with smaller or larger fold widths to create more intricate or interesting patterns.

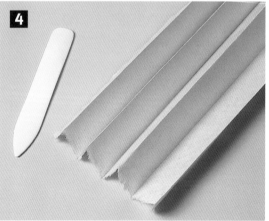

5 Starting at one end of the folded fan, fold the tip into a triangular shape. Crease with a bone folder.

6 Fold the triangle back, and continue to fold back and forth.

7 When all that remains is a little triangular bundle, use a clamp to hold the bundle securely, exposing a corner.

8 Dip the corner of the clamped bundle first into one color of ink, and then into a second color. Repeat with the other two corners, moving the clamp as necessary.

9 Allow to air-dry overnight. Open out the folded abaca to reveal a kaleidoscope of color and pattern.

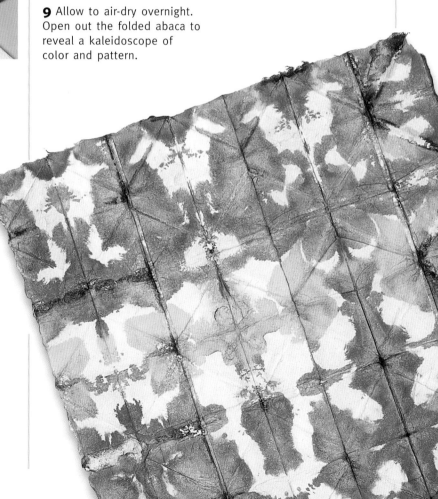

PROJECTS

Music Paper Sheets and Envelopes

Now that you have mastered the skill of sheet formation, you may want to share some of your work with friends in the form of a beautiful letter and envelope combination. Envelopes are formed in the same way as the sheets, by pulling the mold and deckle through the vat of pulp, then couching, pressing, and drying the paper. The difference is simply in the shape of the deckle, and in the folding that occurs after the paper has dried.

There are many sizes and shapes of envelopes but it is a good idea to master the basic form included here.

Sometimes it is possible to peel open a machine-made envelope to use as an outline for your deckle. Modify these instructions to suit your needs and look for a variety of shapes and sizes to use with your own stationery and cards.

On page 25 we suggest using a kitchen spatter-screen to make a circle of paper. This may be folded into an enclosure for a letter by placing the note in the center of the circle and folding in the edges toward the center, then tying with raffia, or sealing with wax or a sticker (see picture above right). We have used a pliable plastic placemat as the material for the envelope deckle. It is sturdy and waterproof, dries easily, and is inexpensive and easy to store. By using this deckle, your envelope will have a deckle edge all around the form. This makes an elegant accompaniment to the handmade paper card enclosed. Alternatively, you can use the cutout section of the placemat to trace an envelope form onto a sheet of paper. If you cut around the edges you will have a perfect envelope form, ready for folding and gluing. This envelope will have a cut, not a deckle edge.

YOU WILL NEED
- shredded office paper
- scissors
- kitchen blender
- music sheets torn into ½ in (1½ cm) pieces
- vat for preparing pulp
- wire whisk
- mold and deckle
- couching pad (see page 26)
- steel ruler
- craft knife
- cutting mat
- sheet of machine-made paper
- plastic placemat
- pen
- sheet of handmade paper, 8½ x 11 in (21 x 28 cm), for handmade envelope
- bone folder
- white glue
- sheet of handmade paper for cut-edge envelope

PREPARING THE MUSIC PULP

1 Cut shredded office paper into 2 in (5 cm) pieces (longer strips will wrap around the blade mechanism of the blender), then blend them with water to make pulp.

2 After the pulp has been blended, add a handful of music pieces and blend for about five seconds, just long enough to incorporate the music pieces thoroughly without destroying their identity.

3 Pour the pulp into a vat of water and whisk briskly to distribute the pulp.

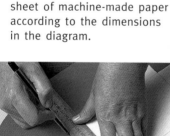

4 Using a deckle, pull the sheet of music paper or envelope form. Watch for holes appearing in the sheet; these may be patched by putting a piece of music sheet in the vat over the hole.

5 Couch the sheet onto a couching pad. Press and dry. This sheet will fold in half to become a small greeting card or thank-you note.

PREPARING THE ENVELOPE DECKLE

This envelope will hold a 3½ x 3½ in (9 x 9 cm) card.

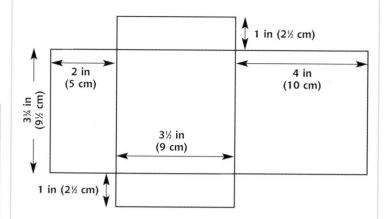

1 in (2½ cm)

2 in (5 cm)

4 in (10 cm)

3¾ in (9½ cm)

3½ in (9 cm)

1 in (2½ cm)

1 Using a steel ruler and craft knife and working on a cutting mat, cut out a plain sheet of machine-made paper according to the dimensions in the diagram.

2 Place the cutout on the center of the plastic placemat and trace around the edges with a pen.

3 Cut the placemat along the lines using a steel ruler and craft knife. Put the cutout piece aside for use in the next envelope. Use the prepared deckle to form a sheet by placing it on top of a 9 x 11 in (22 x 28 cm) mold. Hold firmly together and pull the sheet through the vat of pulp, scooping away extra pulp.

4 When using the envelope deckle be sure to scoop away any extra pulp which collects on the deckle, as this will produce ragged edges, making it difficult to form crisp folds on your envelope.

ASSEMBLING A HANDMADE ENVELOPE

1 Use a bone folder to crease the folded side flaps.

5 After couching, carefully lift the deckle and remove any pieces of music or pulp that may be clinging to the edge of the sheet.

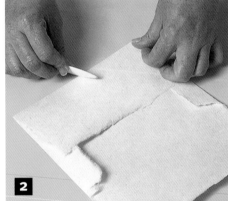

2 Fold the bottom flap up and use the bone folder to produce a clean, folded edge. Glue to secure the edges.

► Musical pieces add a wonderful touch to handmade paper sheets and envelopes.

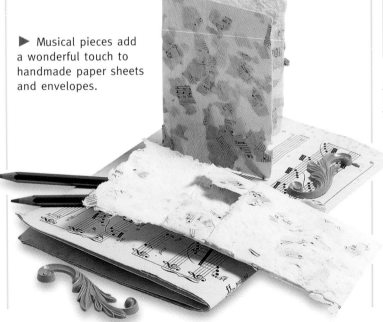

3 Fold the top flap down and crease with the bone folder.

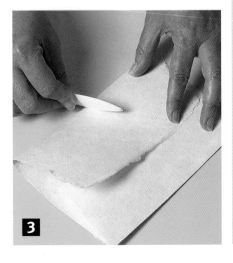

MAKING A CUT EDGE ENVELOPE BY CUTTING A DRY SHEET

1 Trace around the cutout plastic placemat (see earlier) onto a piece of dried handmade paper.

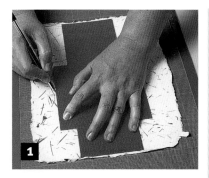

2 Using a steel ruler and craft knife, cut around the outlined shape.

3 Fold the side, bottom, and top edges, creasing with a bone folder.

4 Apply glue to the edges to form an envelope without a deckle edge.

▼ Exquisite deckle-edged envelopes and note cards can be made using the simplest of techniques and ingredients.

► Use different combinations of paper types to make unique card-and-envelope sets.

Papercast Decorations and Favors

There are many ways of turning papercast decorations into significant projects. You can use them to decorate a gift, to hang from a festive tree, to mark the place of guests at dinner, to send home as a remembrance of a special occasion, or to give away as a party or wedding favor.

If you need to make only a small number of papercast objects, you will probably be able to let them air-dry as you make them one at a time. However, if you are preparing for a large number, you will need to use the microwave method. Both methods are outlined on pages 42–43.

YOU WILL NEED
- papercast shapes: shell, butterfly, and star (see pages 42–43)
- gold powder
- small brush
- hole punch
- raffia
- liquid glitter pens
- needle and white cotton thread
- clear glue
- silver glitter
- tray
- white glue
- square of blue abaca paper
- wire loop

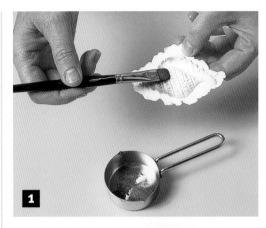

GILT SEASHELL
1 Lightly brush gold powder over the raised edges of the papercast seashell.

2 Punch a small hole in the center of the "top" edge.

3 Insert a piece of raffia through the hole and tie the ends in a tight knot to make a loop for hanging.

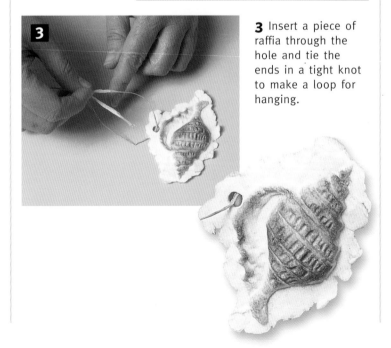

MULTICOLORED BUTTERFLY

1 Using a blue sparkle pen, accent raised lines on the butterfly's wings, ensuring that each wing is symmetrical in its markings. Repeat using a green pen and choosing another set of raised lines on each wing.

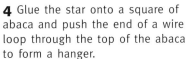

2 Use a gold pen to accent the antennae and the body of the butterfly.

3 Using white cotton thread, pass the needle through the top of the butterfly edge and form a loop for hanging.

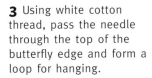

STAR ON INDIGO BACKGROUND

1 Apply clear glue to the raised parts of the star.

2 Holding the star over a tray, sprinkle silver dust onto the star. Shake it to remove any excess sparkle.

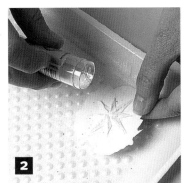

3 Apply white glue to the reverse side of the papercast star, smoothing the glue onto all flat surfaces with your fingertip.

4 Glue the star onto a square of abaca and push the end of a wire loop through the top of the abaca to form a hanger.

◀ Add sparkle and a personal touch to your Christmas tree using snow-white papercast objects set in an endless variety of shapes.

Printing on Handmade Paper

Many people have access to printers and printing tools and enjoy making their own greeting cards and party or wedding invitations. Sometimes, however, they run into difficulties when the time comes to put print to paper. It is quite possible to ruin sheet after sheet of your lovingly made papers in trying to make it work!

To save you time and frustration, this section gives you some general facts and principles for printing on handmade paper. Handmade paper requires special treatment when combined with modern technology. As always, the best advice is to practice and experiment to discover what works best for each project and to keep notes in your Papermaker's Journal (see pages 70–71).

TIP *When making handmade sheets for printing purposes of any kind, couch the sheets on smooth cloths such as cotton sheeting, for a smoother printing surface. The addition of kaolin clay, available at papermaking suppliers, helps to make the surface even smoother as it acts as a filler.*

▶ Experiment with different types of printing to find the one that best suits your paper.

LASER PRINTING

Paper with long fibers and fluffy deckle edges, such as abaca, can cause difficulties for printing for the following reasons:
- It can clog the printer with loose fiber.
- As handmade paper tends to be thicker than laser paper, the toner may not bond properly and can flake off.
- Laser toner can crack if the printed area falls in the crease of a fold.
  Ideally, well-beaten pulp and a clean, tight-fiber paper are preferred for laser printers. Well-sized abaca is our first choice if it is necessary to use a laser printer. You may need to guide paper with a loose deckle edge by hand as it feeds into the printer.

INK JET PRINTING

Papers with rougher surfaces work better on ink jet printers than on laser printers because the ink is deposited on the surface, printing right over petals and other inclusions. Very soft paper may cause problems, with the ink soaking into the paper and spreading. Try doubling the quantity of sizing to make the paper better able to accept the ink on its surface. Watch for clogging of the print head with loose fiber paper and clean the print head more often than usual.

▶ You can design your handmade paper invitations to suit any occasion.

Kindly respond by February 26, 2000

M

persons will attend

Ink jet printers can produce beautiful results when printing text and pictures on textured paper. As with laser printing, guide paper with a loose deckle edge by hand as it feeds into the printer.

CALLIGRAPHY

Add extra sizing to your pulp to make a surface that will not allow the inks to bleed into the paper. Experiment with a variety of nibs and inks and, if using a fine nib, use a light touch to avoid carving into the paper. The new felt-tip pens or roller tips that are available are great for beginners to use. To get you started and help develop your skills in calligraphy, research some of the many books and courses available.

▲ Different calligraphic styles can look stunning on cards and booklets alike.

LETTERPRESS AND SCREENPRINTING

Letterpress and screenprinting provide further options for printing on handmade paper. Letterpress plates make contact with the paper leaving an impression and a slight indentation in the paper. The plates can be damaged when they make contact with an inclusion such as a petal. Screenprinting deposits the ink on the surface of the paper, much like an ink jet printer; the screenprinter places a specially prepared screen on the paper and runs ink over it. Screenprinting prints well over inclusions, but does not always print fonts with fine lines clearly.

▼ Screenprinting is ideal for printing over inclusions, but does not always print fine fonts clearly.

▼ Letterpress printing is useful for printing invitiation letters and notes.

◄ An example of letterpress printing.

Tealight Enclosures

The Japanese have long combined fire and paper to light up the night with enchanting lanterns and shades. Today, you can combine the skill of papermaking with a foolproof design for lighting up your dinner table with these delightful tealight shades.

These instructions are for a 3 x 3 x 6 in (7½ x 7½ x 15 cm) tealight enclosure. Vary the size to make a cluster of lights for the table. Try other paper types and make patterns with a hole punch in a variety of ways. Scale down the size and have individual lights for each dinner guest to enjoy and to take home as a reminder of the evening.

YOU WILL NEED
- abaca paper
- cutting mat
- steel ruler
- craft knife
- pencil
- bone folder
- star punch
- white glue

WARNING
Never leave a candle unattended and always keep the paper of an enclosure well away from the candle flame. Make sure you use paper fire retardant to seal the paper.

1 Place a 8½ x 11 in (21 x 28 cm) sheet of handmade abaca paper on a cutting mat. Using a steel ruler and craft knife, score and tear off a 6 x 11 in (15 x 28 cm) strip.

2 Measure a ½ in (1½ cm) strip along the short edge, and mark it with pencil dots.

3 Fold the edge over and use a bone folder to crease the edge neatly.

4 Fold the paper in half, not including the creased edge. Crease the fold with a bone folder for a sharp edge.

5 Now fold each half in half again. Do this by folding one edge to the center. Crease to form a sharp edge.

8 Apply white glue to the folded flap.

6 Fold the second outside edge to the center and crease well.

9 Seal the edges to form a four-sided box. Place this enclosure over a tealight.

7 Use a star punch to make a star at the top and bottom of each section.

▼ The warm glow of these simple tealight enclosures can bring magical delight to the plainest surroundings.

Bookmarks

How many times have you looked around for something to mark your page in a book and have ended up using anything from a nail file to a grocery bill? Handmade bookmarks make welcome gifts and may be made as simply or as elegantly as you wish.

The bookmarks featured in this project reflect the care and thought that have gone into the making of each one. They are two of our favorite designs, but feel free to experiment with your own ideas. Use different pulp types, or try other ways of tying, such as using thread, ribbon, wire, or leather. Combine these techniques with embossing and laminating for some unique results. Make your bookmarks as mementos of a wedding or other special occasion, as gift tags that will be used beyond the event, or as enclosures in a letter or greeting card. You are sure to come up with endless designs once you begin.

YOU WILL NEED

- blue handmade paper
- steel ruler
- pencil
- craft knife
- bone folder
- medium-weight cream vellum paper
- fine calligraphy felt-tip pen
- rotary cutting board
- hole punch
- raffia
- cotton and petal handmade paper
- wire initial

HANDMADE PAPER WITH VELLUM OVERLAY AND RAFFIA TIE

1 Beginning with an 8½ x 11 in (21 x 28 cm) sheet of blue handmade paper, measure and mark a strip 2 x 8½ in (5 x 21 cm).

2 Using a craft knife and a steel ruler, carefully score a line between the two markings. Do not cut through the paper.

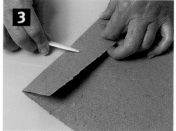

3 Fold the short side in and crease using a bone folder to sharpen the fold.

4 Open out the paper and gently tear along the fold, simulating a deckle edge.

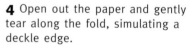

5 Take a sheet of medium-weight cream vellum and, using a fine calligraphy felt-tip pen, put your initials or a design in the bottom corner.

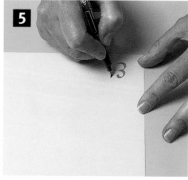

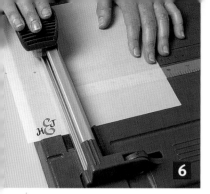

6 Using a rotary cutting board or the craft knife and ruler, cut a strip of vellum slightly narrower and shorter than the base paper to allow the base paper to show around the edges.

7 Holding both pieces of paper together, use a hole punch to make two small holes in the top center, ½ in (1½ cm) from the top edge.

8 Pull a thin piece of raffia about 8 in (20 cm) long through the holes and tie the ends together in a bow. Pull the loops to tighten the bow and flatten it against the bookmark.

COTTON AND PETAL PAPER WITH WIRE INITIAL

1 Begin with a sheet of cotton and petal paper 8½ x 11 in (21 x 28 cm). Measure a strip of paper 8½ x 2½ in (21 x 6 cm). Score and fold as in steps 2 and 3, left.

2 Tear the paper carefully along the folded edge, pulling gently as you tear, and stopping to cut through any petals that are in the way.

3 Push the wire initial through the paper and bend the edges over to hold it firmly.

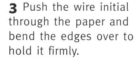

◀ Experiment with different techniques and embellishments to create elegant and original bookmarks for yourself and your friends.

TIP *If a petal peels off and leaves an imprint in the paper, simply apply a spot of glue to the paper, then replace the petal using tweezers.*

Embedded Treasures

Have you been looking for a way to display a few special treasures in a unique way? Why not embed them in pulp to make a unique collection of pieces that may be displayed flat or hung on a wall. Your treasures will be safe and yet visible to be enjoyed by all.

Beach glass—that beautiful by-product of littering that washes up on beaches all over the world—is ideal for displaying along with tiny seashells. You may also want to try embedding twigs, bottle caps, feathers, or tiny bottles; remember to ensure that the pieces are neither too heavy nor too bulky. Try a sample piece like this one, using small shells and glass embedded in plain cotton pulp.

▼ Bring the taste of the outdoors into your home with this delightful collage.

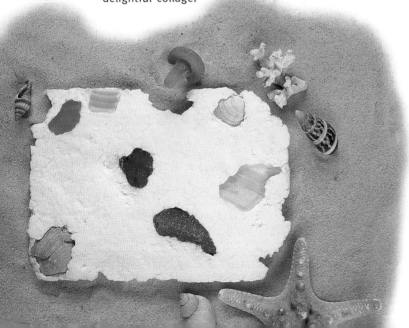

YOU WILL NEED

- collection of small objects, such as glass or shells
- mold and deckle
- shallow tray
- prepared white cotton pulp
- sponge
- knife blade

MAKING A TREASURE DISPLAY

1 Place the mold upside down with the screen side against the table. Arrange the objects to be displayed on the back side of the screen. Remember that they will be seen on the opposite side in the finished piece so place each piece with the display side facing down on the screen.

2 Place the mold screen on a shallow tray to catch excess water from the wet pulp. Taking small amounts of pulp at a time, press the pulp on and around the objects on the mold.

3 Using a sponge, gently press out any extra water from the pulp. This will speed up the drying time. Make sure that you press pulp into all the edges and corners of the mold as some shrinkage will occur.

4 The pulp may take several days to dry. If possible, place it over a fan or air vent to speed up the process. Loosen the edges with a knife, turn the mold over, and gently release the finished piece from the frame.

Molded Bowl

One method of bowl formation involves using prepared pulp, the same as that used for sheet formation, and applying bits of the pulp to the inside of a bowl to cover as desired. Another technique involves placing overlapping layers of pre-formed paper inside the bowl.

Here we use a laminating technique to make wonderful paper bowls which may be left as made or embellished with paint or ink and decorated with threads, feathers, fine wire, beads, and twigs. Once you have discovered the fun of producing these lovely shapes, you will be inspired to try varying the pulp types and colors, the size (use a large salad bowl to make a wonderful decorative or functional bowl), and the embellishments. For this project we have used cotton pulp because of its low-shrinkage quality.

YOU WILL NEED

- cotton pulp that has been prepared and sized
- glass bowls to be used as molds
- sponge
- knife or other fine blade
- pieces of violet-pigmented sheets of handmade paper
- cotton threads
- scissors

BOWLS MADE WITH PROCESSED COTTON PULP

1 Squeeze the excess water out of the pulp so that the pulp is damp but not dripping wet. Taking egg-sized blobs of pulp, press the pulp firmly against the walls of a small glass bowl, covering the entire surface area but leaving the top edge irregular.

2 Press a sponge against the pulp to soak up any extra water. This will cut down on drying time as well as encourage the bonding of the fibers to strengthen the finished product.

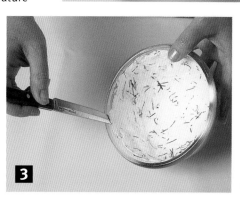

3 Allow the bowl to air-dry. It may take a day or two for the bowl to dry completely. Humidity and temperature will influence the drying time. When the bowl has dried thoroughly, use a knife to loosen carefully the top edge of the bowl.

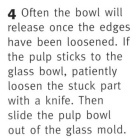

4 Often the bowl will release once the edges have been loosened. If the pulp sticks to the glass bowl, patiently loosen the stuck part with a knife. Then slide the pulp bowl out of the glass mold.

5 The finished bowl should be balanced and shaped exactly like the glass bowl. The outside of the paper bowl will have a smooth surface from being pressed against the glass. The inside will be rougher in texture since it has not been restrained in the drying process.

TIP *For best results, form your pulp bowl on the inside of the bowl being used as your mold. As the pulp fibers dry, they shrink, making it very difficult to remove from the outside of a mold. When formed inside a mold, the edges are easily loosened and the new bowl slips out with a lovely smooth outer texture and a rougher air-dried texture on the inside.*

BOWL MADE WITH HANDMADE PAPER

1 Pull fresh sheets or tear dampened sheets of violet-pigmented handmade paper into pieces about 2 x 3 in (5 x 7½ cm) and apply them in a single layer inside the bowl, over-lapping the edges slightly.

2 Spray the paper with water as you work to keep the paper damp.

3 Keep a sponge handy to press and seal the edges of the paper.

4 Cut two threads long enough to run across the bowl with ends extending about 3 in (7½ cm) beyond the edges. Drape them across the bowl, crossing them in the center.

5 Apply a second layer of damp paper pieces to the entire bowl, covering the threads and any thin spots carefully.

6 Once again, use a sponge to press the paper firmly against the glass bowl and to ensure that all edges are smoothly pressed down.

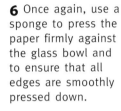

7 When the paper bowl has completely air-dried, loosen the edges with a knife edge, watching out for the threads hanging down. With a larger bowl, there may be places where the pulp has adhered to the glass. Carefully ease the knife blade between the paper and the bowl until the entire form is loosened.

TIP *If you find that the pulp sticks to the bowl, spread the surface with a light coating of petroleum jelly or spray oil prior to applying the pulp.*

8 Lift the finished paper bowl out of the glass bowl.

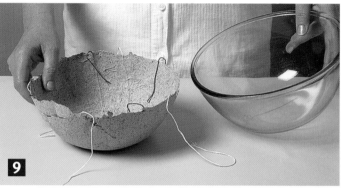

9 The top edge of your paper bowl will be irregular and somewhat delicate. It is now ready to be displayed on a table or hung on a wall. The outside will have a smooth finish while the inside will be more irregular.

▼ The finished bowls can be hung for decorative effect, or filled with glass or chocolates to place on a coffee table.

Wall Hanging

This modular wall hanging has a versatile plan that you may adapt easily to your own specifications. Here three squares have been joined, with the object of hanging them vertically. They could be joined and hung horizontally or more squares could be added in both directions using a variety of pulp shades. A patchwork quilt effect could be achieved by making a sampler of many different squares.

YOU WILL NEED
- vat of plain abaca pulp
- couching surface (see pages 26–27)
- wire whisk
- mold and deckle, 7 x 7 in (18 x 18 cm)
- leaves
- cotton embroidery thread
- blue pigmented abaca pulp
- white glue

For our purposes, we have used abaca pulp for its toughness borne of long fibers, and for its translucency when formed into thin sheets. Since we have couched two sheets together with something in between, this wall hanging looks effective hanging in front of a window or other light source to see this effect.

MAKING THE WALL HANGING

1 Couch a 6 x 6 in (15 x 15 cm) sheet of plain abaca on to the couching pad. Place the leaf in the center of the square.

2 Use dried leaves or foliage that have been dried under weight. Be sure that the leaf lies flat on the newly formed sheet so that the second sheet will adhere to the first. If the leaf is too bulky, it will push the two sheets apart.

3 Place four 18 in (45 cm) lengths of thread along each side of the leaf, 1 in (2½ cm) from the outer edge.

4 Carefully laminate a second sheet on top of the first.

▶ Delicate leaf patterns like this are natural accompaniments to the medium of paper.

5 Lift the mold off without disturbing the threads. Press and dry the squares in the usual way. Make two abaca squares and one blue pigmented square for this wall hanging. Join the pieces together by tying adjacent threads together, leaving an equal distance between squares. Vary the number of squares and the colors and enclosures for an endless array of possibilities. You could even make a paper quilt using many different squares.

▶ Plain deep blue works beautifully for square number two.

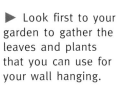

TIP *To transform an 8½ x 11 in (21 x 28 cm) deckle into a 6 in (15 cm) square, use duct tape to define a 6 x 6 in (15 x 15 cm) square on the screen side of the mold. Build up three or four layers of tape to form a deckle that will define the edges of the sheet. Pull the sheet as usual but it is not necessary to use the wooden deckle since the tape acts as a deckle instead. Scoop any extra pulp off the mold before couching and then couch as usual.*

▶ Look first to your garden to gather the leaves and plants that you can use for your wall hanging.

Layered Greeting Cards

Now that you have mastered the process of making envelopes (see pages 50–53), you are ready to take sheet-making a step further. Layering pieces of handmade paper to create a variety of effects allows you an endless number of possibilities for making and giving cards.

YOU WILL NEED
- **3 pieces of paper for the base cards**
- **bone folder**
- **variety of handmade papers for layering**
- **steel ruler**
- **pencil**
- **petal paper heart**
- **needle and white cotton thread**
- **star-shaped hole punch**
- **white glue**

Make several of each kind or make each a unique creation. Try different paper types and colors but always use paper that has been sized in order to have a suitable writing surface. Here are three examples of layered greeting cards. Add your own creativity to these basic techniques and send cards that will be treasured by your friends.

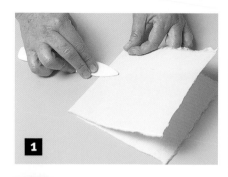

HEART TO HEART

1 Fold a 6 x 12 in (15 x 30 cm) base sheet of paper in half. Use a bone folder to press a sharp fold.

2 Use a sheet of pink handmade paper with white heart confetti as the second layer. Measure and mark the paper so that it is ¼ in (6 mm) less on all sides than the face of the base card. Fold the marked line.

3 Tear, but do not cut, the folded edge to match the deckle edge on the other sides and on the base card. Affix to the base card.

4 Center a petal paper heart on the face of the card. Push a needle with white cotton thread through the heart and the card slightly to the left of the center.

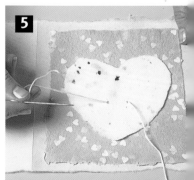

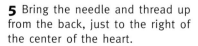

5 Bring the needle and thread up from the back, just to the right of the center of the heart.

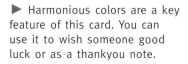

▶ This charming card is difficult to beat, both as a token of love and as a subtle combination of shapes and colors.

5 Punch a star into a 1 in (2½ cm) square of moss green abaca paper and glue it to the other end of the blue piece.

▶ Harmonious colors are a key feature of this card. You can use it to wish someone good luck or as a thankyou note.

STARRY NIGHT

1 For the base sheet, fold a piece of yellow recycled paper in half and crease with a bone folder for a crisp fold.

AU NATUREL

1 Use a piece of black pigmented cotton as the base card. Crease the fold with a bone folder. Tear a piece of textured handmade paper to fit the base card, leaving a ¾ in (2 cm) margin at each side and an ⅛ in (3 mm) margin at the top and bottom. Apply white glue around each edge, smoothing the ridge of glue with a fingertip.

2 Tear a piece of blue handmade paper to measure ¾ in (2 cm) smaller on each side than the face of the card. Then punch a star about ½ in (1½ cm) from the top of the blue piece.

2 Carefully affix it to the base card. Paper made from 100 percent leaves is brittle and easily torn so work carefully and be sure to glue down the edges to prevent them from flaking when handled.

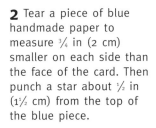

3 Apply a thin line of white glue around the edge of the blue piece.

4 Smooth the glue with a fingertip to prevent the glue from oozing onto the card when affixed. Affix it to the base card.

▲ Use dark-colored natural ingredients for a more rustic look and feel to your card.

Book Pages for Papermaker's Journal

The first time you decide to reproduce a particular paper type, you may discover that the final product is quite different from the original. Approximation and memory are not enough when precision is required.

Even if you are making paper for your own pleasure and never intend to repeat the same recipe, you will still benefit from careful recording. Your Papermaker's Journal will be a guide and history book, showing your growth and development as you add and experiment with new ideas and products. You will also be able to take a recipe that you have developed to new levels.

YOU WILL NEED
- shredded paper
- kitchen blender
- vat for preparing pulp
- wire whisk
- mold and deckle
- couching surface
- printer or photocopier
- paperclips

There are two kinds of pages that will be helpful to include in your journal, and you may also want to keep a couple of blank sheets for inspirational thoughts.

An experiment page will help you work through the trial and error of developing a specific task, to organize and proceed step by step, and to record thoughts and cautions you will want to remember for another time.

EXPERIMENT PAGE

Date:

Purpose:

Method:

Ingredients used:	Quantities:
Sizing	
Pigment 1	
Pigment 2	
Coagulant	
Soda ash	
Pulp type	
Retention agent	
Petal mix	

Conclusion:

The second useful type of page is the recipe sheet. This is exactly like that used in a regular cookbook and it is where you will record the actual, repeatable recipes that you will use over again. Unlike the experiment page, the recipe records specific instructions to a known destination. Clip or staple a swatch of paper to each recipe as a reminder of the texture and color of paper produced by each one.

RECIPE

Name of product:

Procedure:

Ingredients and measurements:

Notes:

MAKING JOURNAL PAGES

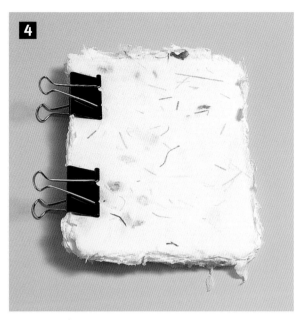

1 Make 25 sheets of 5½ x 8½ in (14 x 21 cm) paper (see pages 24–28). Cotton and abaca with some extra sizing will produce pages that are strong, longlasting, and somewhat resistant to water. This is important because you may need to write something down while your hands are still damp. Press and dry the pages.

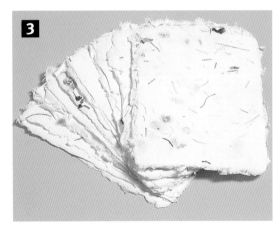

2 Determine the method by which you will print on your pages (see pages 56–57). Hand-printing, using an ink jet printer, or photocopying pages are three good options for this project.

3 Print ten experiment pages and ten recipe pages. Use one blank sheet for your title page and keep the other four blank sheets for writing notes, comments, ideas for future development, or sketches of new designs.

4 When the pages are prepared, arrange them in order and clip along the left-hand side in preparation for binding. Choose one of the binding methods outlined in this book and assemble your Papermaker's Journal.

TIP *An example of a caution from one papermaker's journal is a paragraph at the bottom of an experiment page, beginning, "This paper is a huge pain to make! I found the pulp sticks to the screen, leaving big, gaping holes in every sheet. So, to fix this problem . . ." In writing this caution, the papermaker, was able to express her frustration and to think through and record a solution to the problem.*

CHAPTER 2

Bookbinding Techniques and Projects

BOOKBINDING ALLOWS YOU TO CREATE SOMETHING THAT IS BOTH BEAUTIFUL AND FUNCTIONAL. DESIGNING AND BINDING A SCRAPBOOK IN WHICH TO COLLECT TREASURED PICTURES AND MEMORABILIA, FOR INSTANCE, CAN BRING GREAT PLEASURE AND SATISFACTION. BOOKBINDING ALSO INDULGES A LOVE OF PAPER. PAPER IS AN ESSENTIAL COMPONENT OF BOOKBINDING AND THERE IS DELIGHT TO BE HAD IN SELECTING SPECIFIC COLORS, WEIGHTS, AND TEXTURES THAT PERFECTLY SUIT A BOOKBINDING PROJECT.

TO CREATE BEAUTIFUL AND FUNCTIONAL HANDBOUND BOOKS, SOME EQUIPMENT AND PREPARATORY INFORMATION IS ESSENTIAL. THE FIRST PART OF THIS SECTION DESCRIBES THE TOOLS AND TECHNIQUES OF BOOKBINDING THROUGH DETAILED INSTRUCTIONS AND STEP-BY-STEP PHOTOGRAPHS. THEN, USING THE DIFFERENT TECHNIQUES LEARNED IN THE FIRST PART, YOU CAN ATTEMPT THE WIDE VARIETY OF HANDBOUND BOOKS IN THE PROJECTS SECTION. ABOVE ALL, EXPERIMENT AND HAVE FUN!

BEFORE YOU START

The Parts of the Book

Before you start binding books, there are some standard terms that you will see used throughout the book. Each part of a book has a specific name. Learn the names or mark this page for future reference.

FRONT COVER The front cover, or front board, is the most obvious part of the book. Immediately visible to the reader, the front cover often features decorations, embellishments, the title, and the author's name. Covers can be hard or soft; some of the many available materials for making covers will be discussed in following chapters.

BACK COVER The back cover, or back board, is the necessary partner to the front cover, usually made from the same material with similar styling, even if it is often without the front cover's embellishments and printing.

SPINE The spine connects the front and back covers, while protecting the edges of the inner pages. It is the part of the book that is visible when it is placed on a bookshelf, and may be decorated, featuring exposed bindings, protective fabric, or paper.

TEXT BLOCK Often called the book block, the text block refers to the pages inside the book, either sections, folios, or sheets.

FOLIO Loosely defined, this is any paper folded in half. In hand-bookbinding, folios are often stacked one on top of the other for binding. Each folio has two leaves, and each leaf has two pages, one on each side.

SECTION Placing several folios inside each other creates a section. The resulting edge will be uneven; this can be left as it is, or trimmed to a neat edge.

SIGNATURE The signature is the name given to a section after printing. Most books have multiple signatures.

HEAD AND TAIL The head and tail are the top and bottom of a book, when the book is stood up with the front cover facing forward.

FOREDGE The foredge is the side of the book that opens, usually parallel to the spine.

END PAPER A folded sheet of decorative paper, one leaf of which is pasted to the front or back of a hardcover book. The other leaf is pasted to the first or last page of the book.

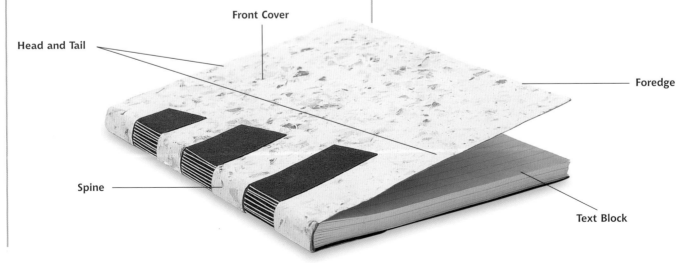

Front Cover

Head and Tail

Foredge

Spine

Text Block

SIDE VIEW OF BOOK

VIEW OF OPENED BOOK

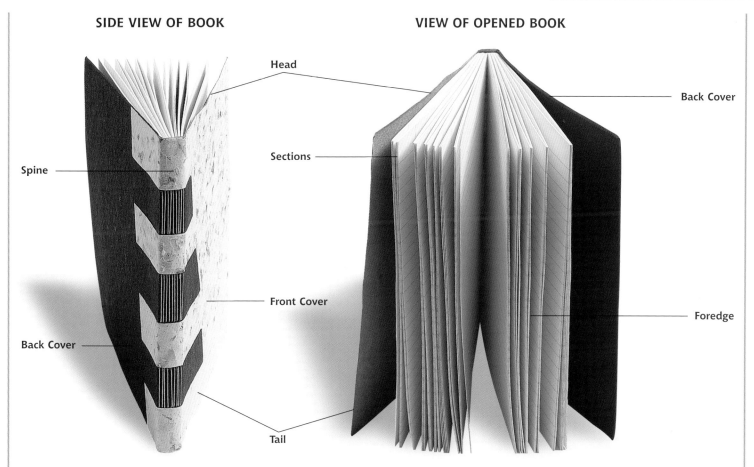

Head

Spine

Back Cover

Front Cover

Tail

Sections

Back Cover

Foredge

TIP *When printing a book, it is easier and more economical to print a large sheet and fold it down with two or more folds. As mentioned already, folding a large sheet into two creates a folio, but the sheet can also be folded into quarters or smaller. Folding into four is called a quarto, and folding once more is called an octavo. The quarto or octavo sections are bound and the edges of the text block are trimmed after binding.*

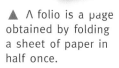

▼ A quarto is a page obtained by folding a sheet of paper in half twice.

▲ A folio is a page obtained by folding a sheet of paper in half once.

◄ An octavo is a page obtained by folding a sheet of paper in half three times.

Materials

Before selecting the materials for your book, consider a variety of factors: what is locally available, what is the overall look desired, and what are the physical requirements of the binding method used? Most of the supplies used in this book came from local craft and hobby supply stores. Suppliers are also listed at the back of the book (see page 156).

As your interest in bookbinding grows, you may want to pick up interesting materials whenever you find them; good examples are papers, threads, ribbons, and book ornaments. Even if you do not have a specific book project planned, it is useful to have a variety of materials available when you begin a new project. Travels to other regions or countries are wonderful for finding special pieces that are not readily available at home.

COVER MATERIALS

For a softcover book, select card stock paper, which is flexible and durable enough to withstand repeated opening and handling. Watercolor paper, printmaking paper, and calligraphy papers work well, as do stiffer handmade papers (especially abaca or hemp) and drawing paper.

Hardcover books require a pliable and sturdy cover material that will be pasted or glued to a board. Look for paper that is thin enough to fold neatly around the corners and produce tight, crisp points and edges. (Very thick paper, such as heavy cotton paper or card stock, will not fold neatly and is difficult to make into a point.)

Book cloth feels like a combination of paper and cloth and is designed specifically for covering book boards. More costly than cloth or paper, book cloth is strong and resilient.

BOARDS

Hardcover books use boards covered with paper or cloth to create a solid front and back cover. Davey board is a brand of heavy board that is sold at most art supply stores and is archival, which means that it remains chemically stable over time. Heavy board ranges in color from gray to brown, and is best covered with a decorative material. Regular cardboard is too thin and vulnerable to piercing to use for bookbinding, but thin wood, metal, and Plexiglass are alternatives that are strong and do not require covering as they are unique in their own right. Book board and poster board are available in many beautiful colors and therefore do not need to be covered. However, these materials may not always be archival.

ADHESIVES

Adhesives are referred to as either pastes or glues. Paste is made from wheat flour and cooked with water to create an inexpensive, effective adhesive. It is archival and slow drying, a characteristic which is very useful when positioning and repositioning book board on a cover. It is applied with a brush and must be refrigerated to prevent spoiling.

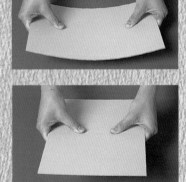

TIP *Most papers and boards have a "grain" which runs from one length of the material to the other. All materials should have their grain running from the head to the tail of a book in order to minimize warping. Test the grain by gently flexing the material. The material will flex the most in the direction of the grain. The topmost picture shows the board flexing more than in the lower picture, therefore the grain runs up and down the short length of the board.*

Glues include white glue, other synthetic adhesives, and animal adhesives (made from hides and bones). White glue is the glue used in the techniques and projects in this book, as it is quick-drying and an excellent complement to wheat paste. Store white glue in a small cone-topped bottle for handy application and airtight storage. Apply glue with a brush or plastic trowel. White glue can be archival; check with your supplier.

BINDING MATERIALS

There are many options when selecting a binding material. Colorful embroidery threads, ribbon, waxed linen thread, wire, and post-and-screw are all materials which will appear in the techniques and projects of this book.

Select a material that best suits the overall look and functionality of the book. For a sewn section book, a thin, strong bookbinding thread will secure the sections tightly. For a photo album, where pages may be added or removed, use a tied ribbon or post-and-screw binding. For a natural look, use raffia or copper wire.

Avoid using binding materials that might stretch or break during binding. For this reason it is best to avoid using elastic cord, sewing thread, or the curly plastic ribbon used in wrapping gifts. Look instead for waxed linen thread in the beading section of your local craft store.

WAX

Coating binding thread with a thin layer of wax helps the thread to pass through the holes smoothly and makes it grip the paper once in place. Use a simple ball of beeswax, found in the quilting section of a craft store, and pull the thread through the wax two or three times. Decorative ribbons should not be waxed, while embroidery and bookbinding threads should.

TIP *Some papers, boards, and pastes are archival. This means that they have a neutral pH and should remain chemically stable over time. In order to produce an archival book, each and every component of the book must be archival. Not all books must be archival, however. Assess the nature of your project and decide whether archival is important. Projects such as photo albums have such lasting value that you will want them to be made of the most enduring materials.*

Tools

Good tools are essential for bookbinding because they directly affect the results. If you buy a cheap paste brush, for example, you will find that it loses hairs in the paste and on the covers.

Likewise, low-quality cutting tools can waver and produce incorrectly cut paper. All of this has been learned by experience, and it is recommended that you buy the best tools that you can afford. When starting out in bookbinding, you may not be able to purchase all of the tools shown in this book. But starting with the basics will allow you to begin creating wonderful handbound books, and other equipment can always be purchased later.

YOU WILL NEED

To begin bookbinding, you will need the following tools:

- exacto cutting knife with blades
- straight ruler with metal edge
- bone folder
- bookbinding or embroidery needle
- paste brush
- brayer (small roller)
- awl
- hammer
- pencil
- scrap or paste paper
- press for pasted books, made of two boards and four G-clamps
- scissors
- cutting mat
- metal clips

Other items that are useful to have include:

- **Craft drill for drilling small to large holes through bookbinding board and text blocks.**
- **Rotary cutting board, as shown in this book, or paper cutter with safety arm for cutting several sheets of paper at a time. The blades may be sharpened or replaced as needed.**
- **Traditional bookbinder's press with crank wheel. Easier to operate than a board and G-clamp press, but less portable because it is very heavy.**
- **Triangle to measure and produce right angles.**

Rotary cutting board

BOOKBINDING LOCATION

When selecting a location for bookbinding, it is important to find a place that will inspire your creativity. You may even want to alternate between two locations. Perhaps you have a space that is dedicated to bookbinding, or perhaps you use a workspace that is also used for other purposes. Either way, having sufficient working space, and materials and tools close by is very important.

CHECKLIST:

- Store tools in tins or plastic containers that are portable and easy to store.
- Keep paper flat and in a cool, dry place to prevent it curling.
- Your work area should be large enough for your cutting mat and paper size (working with large sheets of paper requires a larger work area).
- Give yourself plenty of elbow room when cutting and hammering.
- Keep adhesives, knives, needles, and metal objects safely stored away from the reach of children.

TIP Replace the blade of a cutting knife frequently to maximize safety. A dull blade will require more pressure to cut through the material, which can lead to the wavering or jumping of the blade.

BASIC TECHNIQUES

Making a handbound book requires the knowledge of a variety of basic techniques, which are repeated in the process of designing a well-made piece. Mastering these techniques will help you create a book that will hold together and last.

Using the tools described on the previous page, familiarize yourself with the techniques by practicing on scrap paper. Save your practice pieces to remember the steps as you move onto the project section of this book.

FOLDING

1 When folding paper for bookbinding, always use a bone folder to make a crisp folded edge. Bring one edge of the paper over to the other edge. Press the bone folder into the center of the folded edge and move it outward, pressing firmly to flatten one half of the fold.

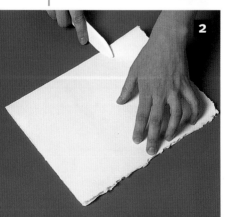

2 Return the bone folder to the center of the fold and run it over the other half of the fold, moving out from the center, creating a crisp edge all along the edge of the fold. Use this technique when folding a single page (as shown) or several pages in a section.

CUTTING

1 Trim a set of pages using a paper cutter. The paper cutter shown here uses a rotary blade that holds the papers in place and safely cuts along the outer edge. Place the paper(s) under the metal bar, lower the bar, and position the cutting mechanism at the top of the bar. Press down on the mechanism and pull down in a steady, swift manner, trimming the pages to the desired width.

2 Use a steel ruler and cutting blade in the same manner, pulling the blade from top to bottom along the edge of the ruler.

TIP *For the greatest amount of control and safety, always trim paper by pulling the blade toward the body. Cutting across the body places the arm in an awkward position, which can lead to dangerous wobbling and loss of control.*

SCORING

1 To create a score for folding, first mark the start and end points for the score with a sharp pencil.

2 Line up a ruler to the marks. Hold the bone folder like a pencil and press down at the top of the ruler. Pull the bone folder toward your body in a steady manner, applying even pressure to the paper.

PIERCING AND PUNCHING

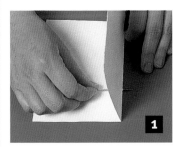

1 Pierce holes in paper by using a bookbinder's needle. First mark the holes then pierce each mark with the needle, pressing firmly but gently into the paper. This method works best with a small number of sheets.

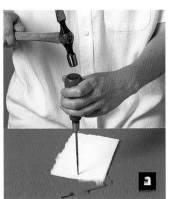

2 For larger holes or thicker stacks of paper, use an awl to punch the holes. Place the item to be punched on a pad to protect your working surface. Position the awl at a 90° angle to the text block, and hit the awl firmly with a hammer. Select a thicker awl for raffia, heavy cord, and leather thong bindings, and thinner awls for ribbon and thread bindings.

TIP *Another excellent method of creating holes in a text block is to use a craft drill. Available at craft and hobby stores, the craft drill is hand-operated and it will easily drill through bookbinding boards and thick text blocks. Select a drill bit to match the width of your binding material.*

APPLYING ADHESIVES

1 Apply adhesives using a plastic or metal trowel, starting from the center of the paper and moving out toward the edges.

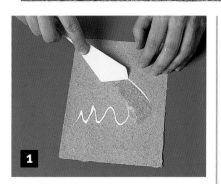

2 Apply paste using a clean brush, placing the paste in the center of the paper and spreading it to the edges.

PREPARING THE TEXT BLOCK

1 To create an evenly aligned stack of paper, jog the text block into alignment by tapping it firmly along the head of the stack, and then along the foredge.

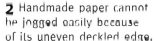

2 Handmade paper cannot be jogged easily because of its uneven deckled edge. To prepare a stack of handmade paper for binding, place each piece on top of another, lining up the binding edge as closely as possible.

MAKING COVERS

Making a Soft Cover

Consider the purpose and binding method of the book when choosing whether to use a soft or hard cover. Some binding methods are more suited to a soft cover, such as the buttonhole stitch. Others work well with either a soft or hard cover, such as the Japanese or stab binding method.

YOU WILL NEED
- card-weight paper
- ruler
- pencil
- craft knife
- metal-edged ruler
- white glue
- brayer (small roller), optional

▼ An endless variety of papers is available for soft covers.

1 Choose the paper for your cover. Card-weight paper is excellent for preparing a softcover book. Several books in the Projects section use card-weight paper. Many options exist, including: poster board; textured papers from specialty paper stores; heavy handmade papers, which are made by adding extra pulp to the vat in order to pull very thick sheets; and corrugated cardboard with an exposed flute, available in a range of flute designs (wavy, zigzag, straight) and colors.

2 To prepare a softcover for a pamphlet book, first measure the dimensions of the pamphlet section.

3 Mark the dimensions on the cover paper. Select a paper that is flexible enough to fold, but strong enough to withstand use.

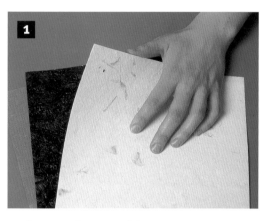

4 Using a craft knife and ruler with a metal edge, trim the paper to the marked dimensions.

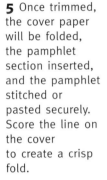

5 Once trimmed, the cover paper will be folded, the pamphlet section inserted, and the pamphlet stitched or pasted securely. Score the line on the cover to create a crisp fold.

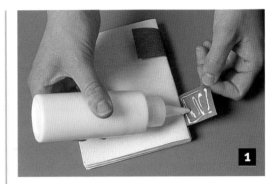

BINDING ON TAPES

1 You can apply a card-weight cover to a text block by applying glue to the tapes of a sewn section, as shown here (see page 94 for sewing technique with tapes).

2 Position the card-weight cover beneath the tapes and press the tapes down. Smooth with fingers or a brayer.

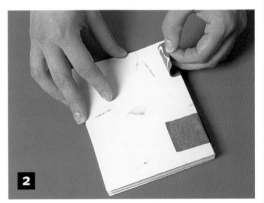

6 Fold along the scored line. This cover is now suitable for being sewn on a pamphlet book.

◀ You can add the perfect finishing touch to your soft cover with a ribbon and seal.

Making a Hard Cover

Before making a hard cover think about the message you are trying to convey. A hard cover imparts a more formal appearance to a book than a soft cover. It protects delicate inside pages and helps to keep the book closed. Hard covers may therefore be more suited to a book with many pages.

YOU WILL NEED
- heavy-weight bookbinding board
- craft knife
- metal-edged ruler
- 2 sheets of natural abaca paper
- 2 sheets of moss-green abaca paper
- pencil
- wheat paste
- small brush
- brayer (small roller)
- bone folder
- waxed paper, flat board, and bricks

TIP *Cover your work surface with plenty of fresh paper, and change the paper frequently to avoid getting paste on the good side of the cover.*

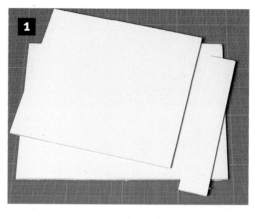

1 Using a craft knife and metal-edged ruler, cut the heavy-weight bookbinding board into three pieces: a back cover measuring 5 x 7 in (12 x 18 cm), a front cover measuring 5 x 5½ in (12 x 14 cm), and a front spine measuring 5 x 1 in (12 x 2½ cm). Using a metal-edged ruler, trim the board for the back cover. Trim the front cover and spine piece to fit the text block.

2 Place the natural abaca covering paper on the work surface, with the right side facing down. Place the back cover on the paper and draw around the edge with a pencil. This outline will give you a guide for positioning the front cover and spine pieces. Trim the excess paper leaving 1–2 in (2½–5 cm) around the edge of the cover marking.

TIP *Determine the cover size by measuring the text block and adding ¼ in (6 mm) to the length and width. This will give enough space to protect the text block and produce a well-proportioned book.*

3 Practice positioning the front cover and spine by first placing the front cover on the paper. Position it within the traced back cover, flush with the right-hand side. Now place the spine flush with the left-hand side. This should leave a gap between the front cover and spine of around ½ in (1½ cm). This gap will later become the hinge of the book.

6 Place the spine onto the pasted paper.

7 Flip the piece over and smooth the paper with a brayer, rolling it from the center of the cover to the outer edges. Continue until the paper is free of air bubbles and creases.

4 Apply wheat paste to the natural abaca cover paper, spreading it from the center of the paper to the outer edges.

5 Place the front cover carefully on the pasted paper.

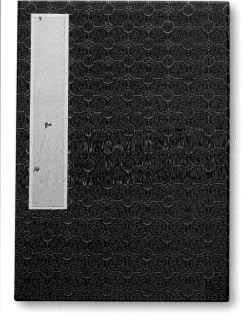

▲ The use of hard covers can give books added definition and elegance.

COMPLETING THE HARD COVER

1 With the cover-board-side up, apply wheat paste to the edges and corners of the paper.

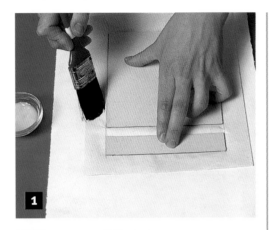

2 Miter the corners by folding each corner to a 45° angle.

3 Apply paste to the edges of the cover paper.

4 Use a bone folder to wrap the paper tightly around the edges. Carefully pull the paper taut and smooth it onto the back of the cover.

5 Fold the spine edge toward the center and smooth the edge with a bone folder.

TIP *When the cover paper is pasted, it will become wet and more fragile than when dry. Be careful when pulling the paper around the edge of a cover, as too much strength can cause the paper to tear. This is especially true when mitering the corners.*

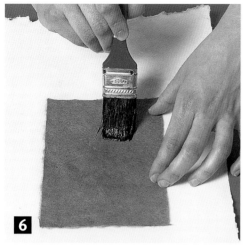

6 Use the moss-green abaca paper to paste onto the inside of the cover. Cut the paper to cover most of the inner cover with a ¼–½ in (6–12 mm) margin. Brush paste onto the inside cover paper.

9 Place the wet cover between layers of waxed paper and flat board. Weigh with bricks and leave for 24 hours.

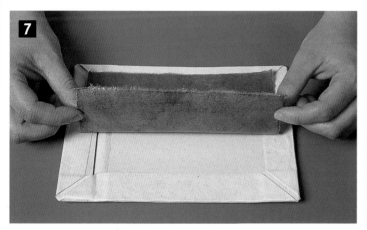

7 Position the paper on the back of the cover.

▶ You can use the hard covers to make a stylish stab-bound book like this (see pages 98–99).

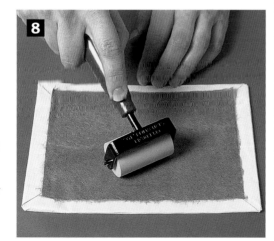

8 Use a brayer to smooth the paper, rolling from the center toward the outer edge.

TIP *Leaving the wet covers to air-dry without pressing leads to warping. Prevent warping by weighing covers under bricks or in a bookbinding press.*

BINDING

Pamphlet Sewing

Pamphlet stitch, one of the simplest methods of binding, is based on three holes. The thread can be hidden or visible as part of the design.

YOU WILL NEED
- paper for pages
- bone folder
- ruler
- pencil
- bookbinder's needle
- cutting mat
- embroidery thread
- scissors

Pamphlet binding can be fastened together with colored embroidery thread, cord, ribbon, raffia, and even shoelaces. Select a sewing needle with a thickness similar to the thread to be used on the book. Thicker sewing materials, such as leather cord or heavy ribbon, will need a thicker needle with a larger eye. Sew a cover and inner pages together to create a quick and easy handbound book. Or create a decorative cover to be added to the section after binding.

MAKING A 3-HOLE SINGLE-SECTION NOTEBOOK

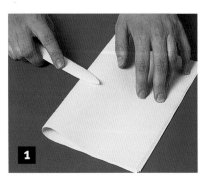

1 Jog several 8½ x 11 in (21 x 28 cm) sheets of paper into alignment. Fold them in half using a bone folder to create a sharp crease.

2 Measure the center point along the fold and mark its position. Measure two holes, 2¼ in (5½ cm) on either side of the center hole, along the fold.

3 Pierce each of the three holes using a bookbinder's needle. Work on a cutting mat to protect your work surface.

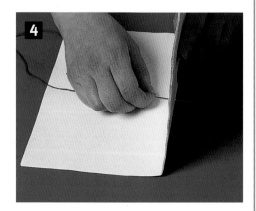

4 Thread the needle with colorful waxed embroidery thread, then push the needle through the center hole from the inside of the pamphlet.

TIP *Splay the ends of the knot after trimming to reduce the chances of the knot coming undone.*

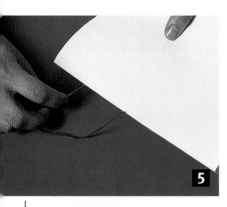

5 Pull the needle and thread out, leaving a 3 in (7½ cm) tail inside the pamphlet. Thread the needle into the top hole, pulling it through to the inside of the pamphlet. Pull until taut.

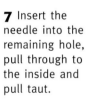

6 Push the needle through the center hole again and exit on the outside of the pamphlet. Pull the thread until it is taut.

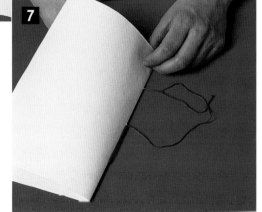

7 Insert the needle into the remaining hole, pull through to the inside and pull taut.

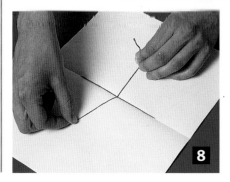

8 Tie a double knot with embroidery thread at the center of the stitching. Use the remaining thread and the tail from the beginning of sewing. Trim the thread with scissors, leaving ½ in (1½ cm) ends.

9 Reverse the sewing to create a decorative bow on the outer spine of the pamphlet. Enter the center hole from the outside instead of the inside, and continue sewing as instructed. The points of entrance will be reversed at every step.

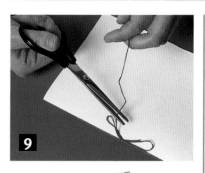

► This pamphlet can make a lovely gift for a friend or a notebook for your personal notes.

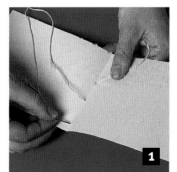

MAKING A 4-HOLE SINGLE-SECTION NOTEBOOK

1 Follow steps 1–3 (left), but measure and pierce four holes instead of three. You will have two center holes and two end holes. Begin sewing at one center hole. Enter the hole from the inside, leaving a 3 in (7½ cm) tail. Pull the thread through the hole and enter the other center hole from the outside. After pulling the thread through, enter the top end hole from inside the pamphlet.

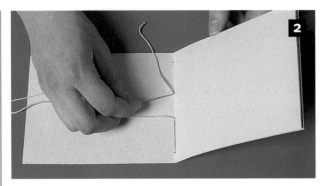

2 Pull the thread through to the outside and enter the nearest center hole. Pull the thread through and enter the other center hole, as shown.

3 Pull the needle and thread through the end hole and tie a knot inside the pamphlet, at the center hole where the sewing began.

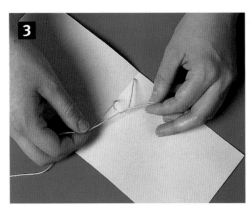

5-HOLE PAMPHLET STITCHING

This variation of the three-hole pamphlet stitch solidly anchors the pages of the section and gives more visual interest with the additional holes. Use the five-hole stitch when working with large pages that need greater stability, or when using the binding threads as decoration. Beading along the exterior spine looks especially lovely with the five-hole stitch.

1 Fold a pamphlet of eight pages in half. Crease with a bone folder. Measure and mark five holes along the fold, with a center hole and two holes on either side. Pierce the holes with a bookbinder's needle.

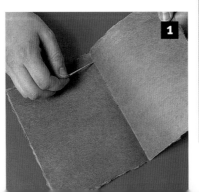

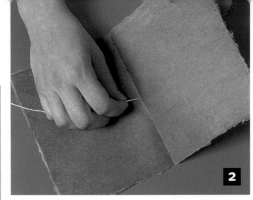

2 Thread a bookbinder's needle with embroidery thread. Pull the needle and thread through the center hole, starting from inside the pamphlet. Pull the thread through, leaving a 3 in (7½ cm) tail.

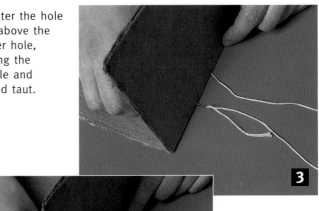

3 Enter the hole just above the center hole, pulling the needle and thread taut.

4 Push the needle through the end hole, from the inside to the outside of the pamphlet.

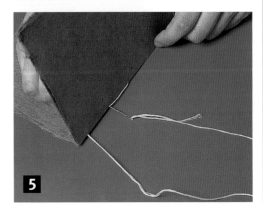

5 Enter the hole just below the end hole, and pull the thread taut to the inside of the pamphlet.

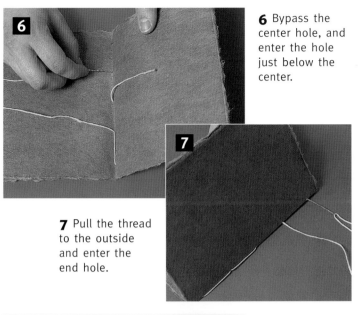

6 Bypass the center hole, and enter the hole just below the center.

10 Tie a knot at the center hole.

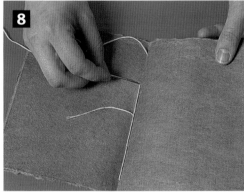

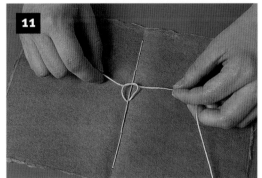

7 Pull the thread to the outside and enter the end hole.

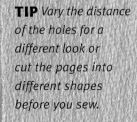

11 To hold the knot securely in place, tie a second knot over the first.

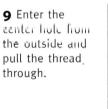

8 In the inside of the pamphlet, push the needle into the hole second from the end.

▶ The five-hole pamphlet stitch is useful for books with large pages. If the book is really big, you can increase the number of holes.

9 Enter the center hole from the outside and pull the thread through.

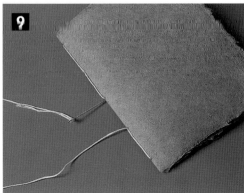

TIP *Vary the distance of the holes for a different look or cut the pages into different shapes before you sew.*

Fold Books

Making fold books is fun and easy to do. Because they do not require pasting, fold books can be made from virtually any sheet of paper. The basic pattern creates squares on a page which are then cut in a circular manner, as shown in the step-by-step photos.

YOU WILL NEED
• handmade paper for folding
• bone folder

However, other cutting patterns may be made to create a fold book with surprising folds and turns. Use your imagination to come up with other patterns! Use paper with enough strength to withstand the multiple folds. Abaca paper is recommended because the long fibers allow for crisp folds and enough strength to withstand folding and cutting. Medium-weight poster board, bond paper, and craft paper each have different weights and each will produce a unique fold book.

1 Select a sheet of paper for folding. These photos show abaca paper in 11½ x 11½ in (29 x 29 cm) size. Fold the paper in half using a bone folder to create a crisp foldline.

2 Now open out the paper and fold each of the halves in half again, to create a paper folded into four strips.

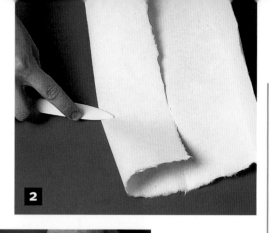

3 Open the paper out, turn it, and fold it in half in the other direction, creating eight folded boxes on the page.

4 Fold each of the halves in half again, as in step 2. The paper will now have three folds running left to right and three folds running top to bottom.

5 Begin tearing the page along the top left row, as shown. Stop before tearing through the last square (see next picture). The idea is to tear the paper into one continuous strip.

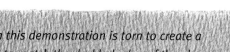

6 Turn the corner, and tear along the next row. Stop at the last square and turn the corner again.

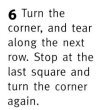

7 Continue tearing in this manner until the entire sheet is torn into a continuous strip.

8 Beginning at the first square, fold the book up, square by square.

▲ A basic fold book.

TIP *The paper in this demonstration is torn to create a deckle-like edge, to match the deckled edge of the abaca paper. When using a machine-made paper with cut edges, replace hand-tearing with a ruler and cutting blade.*

ALTERNATIVE IDEAS

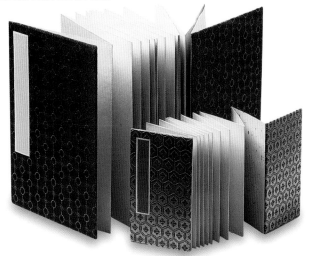

▲ You can paste hard covers to your fold book to give it a more structured, formal feel.

▼ The pages of a fold book are a wonderful way of displaying a store of memories at a glance.

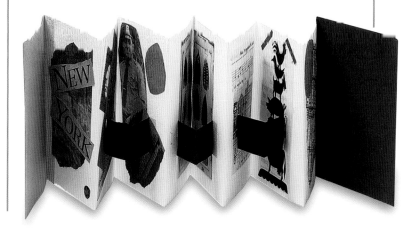

Binding on Tapes and Ribbons

Binding on tapes or ribbons gives the bookbinder some attractive options for embellishing and decorating books. The actual tapes can be decorative papers, ribbons, or bookbinding tape. Once bound, the tapes can be hidden or left exposed, either pasted onto a front and back cover, or decoratively woven into the cover material.

In this review of the technique, the binding will be left unpasted. Look to page 83 for an example of binding on tapes.

YOU WILL NEED

- brick
- paper
- 24 sheets of paper, 5½ x 8½ in (14 x 21 cm)
- bone folder
- sheet of colored paper
- craft knife or scissors
- ruler
- pencil
- clip
- bookbinder's needle
- waxed linen thread
- bookbinding tape

1 Wrap a brick in protective paper. The brick will be used for pressing sections for this book.

2 Fold 24 sheets of 8½ x 5½ in (21 x 14 cm) paper into six sections of four sheets each. Crease with a bone folder.

3 Stack the sections on top of each other and place on a flat surface. Place the wrapped brick on top of the pile of sections and leave for three to four hours to form a tight fold in each section.

TIP *For a larger book, increase the number of tapes to anchor the sections and binding securely.*

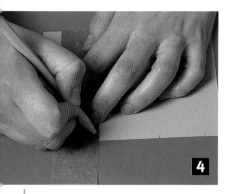

4 Take a sheet of colored paper and cut it to the same length as the length of the section spine. The paper does not have to be the same width, as it will be used for a template for piercing the holes. Measure the width of the tapes onto which you will be sewing; in this case they are 1⅜ in (3½ cm) wide. Mark the placement of the first tape starting ½ in (1½ cm) from the top of the spine. Make a second mark 1⅜ in (3½ cm) from the first mark, indicating the width of the tape. Repeat the step for the second tape, making a mark ½ in (1½ cm) from the bottom of the spine and then 1⅜ in (3½ cm) from that mark, to indicate the width of the tapes. These four marks will show where to pierce the holes for binding.

5 Clip the template to the stack of sections, ensuring that the sections and template are flush with the edge of the spine. Using a pencil and ruler, draw straight lines down the side of the spine, following the marks made on the template, to indicate the holes for piercing.

6 Using a bookbinder's needle, pierce holes in each section, where marked in step 5. Pierce all the sections to prepare for sewing.

Holes 1–4
(left to right)

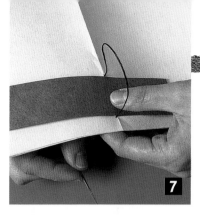

9 Push the needle through hole No.3 and exit to the outside of the section.

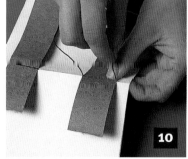

11 Pull the thread through hole No.3 for a second time.

7 Thread the bookbinder's needle with 30 in (75 cm) of waxed linen thread. Begin sewing by passing the needle through hole No.2 from the inside. Exit hole No.2 and enter hole No.1 from the outside. Place the tape in position between the two holes as you pull the thread taut, to hold the tape in place.

8 Tie a double knot over hole No.2 to secure the thread. Note that the book is turned in this photograph.

10 Place the second tape in position and pull the thread taut as you enter hole No.4, as in step 7.

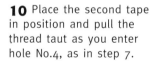

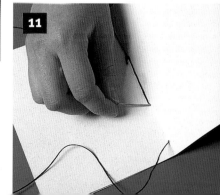

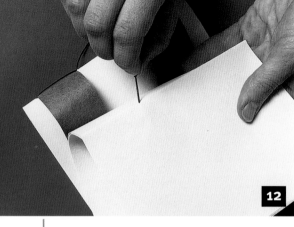

12 Place the next section on top of the first and push the needle through hole No.3 of this new section.

12

13 Pull the needle through hole No.4 to the outside and position the tape.

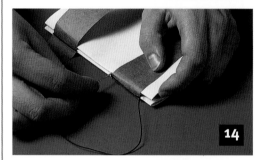

13

14 Enter hole No.3 again and pull the needle through, pulling the thread taut.

14

15 Pull the needle through hole No.2 to the outside. Exit the section and loop the thread around the tape; enter hole No.1 to the inside of the section and exit via hole No.2.

15

TIP *For additional anchoring of sections, loop the needle into the thread of the previous section.*

16

16 Add the third section by entering hole No.2 of the new section. Follow the same pattern described above and continue adding sections until they are all in place.

17 When all the sections are in place, tie a double knot flush with the center hole. Trim the ends of the knot to ½ in (1½ cm).

17

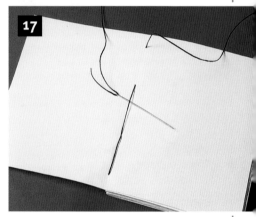

Post and Screw Binding

The post and screw binding is suitable for scrapbooks as it allows pages to be added and removed after binding. The post and screw can be used in cases where such flexibility is desired.

The post and screw mechanism is usually available in copper or silver tones and in a variety of sizes. When making the holes, select a drill bit or awl that is slightly smaller than the post and screw. This will create a hole that remains tight once the post is inserted.

When creating a large scrapbook, try positioning the posts and screws to match the holes of a standard three-hole punch. This will make it simple to punch and add new sheets.

YOU WILL NEED
- handmade paper for text block 4 x 5⅛ in (10 x 12½ cm)
- handmade soft cover
- soft lead pencil
- ruler
- 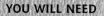 hammer or craft drill
- padding
- posts and screws

1 Prepare the text block and cover for punching. Here, we have selected sheets of 4 x 5⅛ in (10 x 12½ cm) handmade paper and a blue handmade soft cover.

2 Using a soft lead pencil and ruler for accuracy, measure and mark two holes on the outer cover of the book.

3 Hammer or drill the marked holes, protecting the work surface with padding.

4 Insert a post in one hole, then turn the book over and twist in the screw from the other side. Repeat with the second hole.

Stab Binding

Stab binding, which is often referred to as Japanese binding, is traditionally paired with two separate covers and single or folded inner pages. Covers can be made using pasted bookbinding boards with a pasted hinge, or card stock with a scored hinge.

Many different binding patterns exist, including the tortoiseshell and hemp leaf, each with its own unique story and rich heritage. Try this basic five-hole Japanese binding first.

This standard binding works well on books of all sizes. Holes may be punched with an awl and hammer, or drilled with a craft drill and fine bit.

YOU WILL NEED
- scrap paper
- scissors
- ruler
- handmade paper for text block
- clip
- awl
- hammer
- bookbinder's needle
- waxed thread, raffia, or ribbon

TIP *Since the binding and knotting are all external, it is best to start with extra thread to avoid having to tie on a second piece midway through the piece. Five-hole binding usually requires thread five times the height of the book block.*

1 Create a template by trimming a piece of scrap paper to the length of the book spine. Mark five holes ½ in (1½ cm) from the long edge of the spine, with a center hole and two holes on either side.

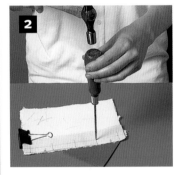

2 Clip the template to the stack of papers for binding. Here we are using five sheets of handmade cotton and gold thread paper. Place the clipped stack onto a protective surface and pierce the holes using an awl and hammer.

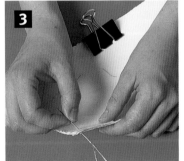

3 Thread a bookbinder's needle with waxed thread, raffia, or ribbon. Here we are using a thin strand of raffia. Begin sewing by entering hole No.1 from the back of the book, and pulling through until a tail of 2 in (5 cm) remains.

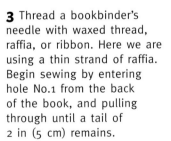

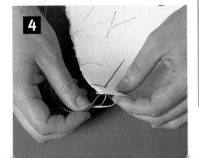

4 Loop the raffia around the head (top) of the book and enter hole No.1 from the back. Loop the raffia around the spine of the book and enter hole No.1 for a third time. Pull the raffia taut.

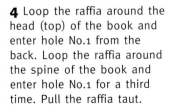

5 Enter hole No.2 from the front and pull the raffia through to the back.

Template for steps 1–15

6 Loop it around the spine of the book and enter hole No.2 for a second time. Pull taut.

9 Enter hole No.4 from the front and pull the raffia to the back.

7 Enter hole No.3 from the back and pull the raffia through to the front.

10 Loop the raffia around and enter hole No.4, pulling the raffia taut.

8 Loop the raffia around the spine of the book and again enter hole No.3. Pull the raffia taut.

11 Enter hole No.5 at the tail of the book from the back. Loop the raffia around the tail of the book and enter hole No.5 again. Loop the raffia around the spine of the book and enter hole No.5 for a third time.

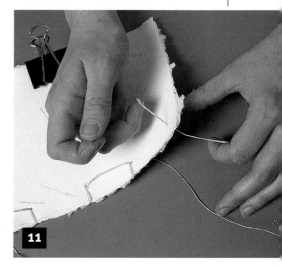

TIP *When using a narrow piece of paper as a template, it is easy to forget which edge is the spine edge. Avoid this situation by marking an arrow pointing toward the spine edge.*

12 This and the following steps will involve sewing back up to the head of the book, filling in the spaces left on the first pass. All sewing at this point will be done from hole to hole, with no looping around the spine. Enter hole No.4 from the front and pull to the back.

13 Enter hole No.3 from the back and pull the raffia through.

14 Enter hole No.2 from the front and pull to the back.

15 Tie a double knot to complete.

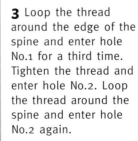

ADVANCED STITCH

There are many decorative variations on the basic stab binding. Each style involves a different number of holes with varied placement. Here the hemp leaf binding is demonstrated.

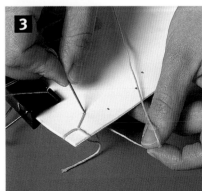

1 Create a template and hammer nine holes in a text block. Note the position of the holes: Nos.1, 3, 4, 6, 7, and 9 are ½ in (1½ cm) from the edge; Nos.2, 5, and 8 are ¾ in (2 cm) from the edge; and holes No.1-2-3, 4-5-6, and 7-8-9 are grouped together. Pull a bookbinder's needle threaded with embroidery or bookbinding thread through hole No.1 from the back. Leave a 2–3 in (5–7½ cm) tail at the back.

2 Loop the thread around the head of the book and enter hole No.1. Pull the thread taut.

3 Loop the thread around the edge of the spine and enter hole No.1 for a third time. Tighten the thread and enter hole No.2. Loop the thread around the spine and enter hole No.2 again.

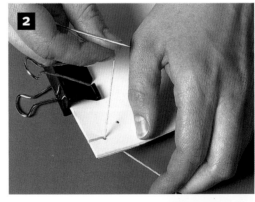

Template for steps 1–7

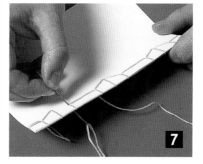

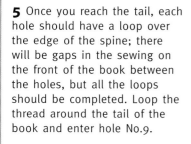

4 Enter hole No.3 from the back and pull through to the front. Loop the thread around the spine and enter hole No.3 again. Continue sewing and looping in a similar manner for holes Nos.4–9.

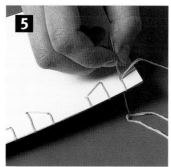

7 Continue sewing from hole to hole until you reach hole No.3, as shown. Pull the thread through hole No.3 to the front. Pull the thread through hole No.2 to the back and tie off with the starting tail using a double knot.

5 Once you reach the tail, each hole should have a loop over the edge of the spine; there will be gaps in the sewing on the front of the book between the holes, but all the loops should be completed. Loop the thread around the tail of the book and enter hole No.9.

◀ ▲ ▼ Stab binding is a distinctive and highly attractive way of adorning your book covers.

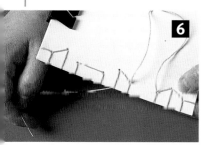

6 Enter hole No.8 from the front and pull the needle through to the back. Enter hole No.7 and pull through to the front. Enter hole No.6 from the front and pull to the back.

TIP For the first sewing pass from head to tail, you will always loop around the spine at each hole, regardless of the number and position of holes.

Buttonhole Stitch

The buttonhole stitch method of binding uses multiple basic sections, as shown in the three-hole pamphlet stitch section (see pages 88–89), sewn around a one-piece cover. The cover is cut from a piece of decorative card stock that is trimmed to fit the number of sections.

This style of binding produces an attractive book that lies flat when opened. A disadvantage of this style is that the binding threads and inner sections are exposed along the spine, which, if exposed to wear and tear, can make the book look worn and compromise the binding.

YOU WILL NEED
- **40 sheets of handmade paper, 4¼ x 11 in (10½ x 28 cm)**
- **bone folder**
- **brick wrapped in paper**
- **clip**
- **craft knife**
- **steel ruler**
- **cutting mat**
- **decorative card stock**
- **pencil**
- **bookbinder's needle**
- **embroidery thread**

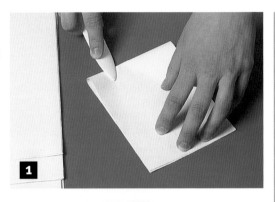

1 Fold in half five sections, each consisting of eight sheets of 4¼ x 11 in (10½ x 28 cm) paper. Use a bone folder to make a sharp crease.

2 Place the sections in a stack and place under a wrapped brick for three to four hours. Clip the sections together; trim the foredge using a craft knife and steel ruler. Work on a cutting mat to protect the work surface.

TIP *Leave the text block untrimmed for a rougher look.*

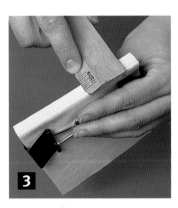

3 Measure the width of the text block; it will be around ⅜ in (9 mm) thick, depending on the weight of the book pages.

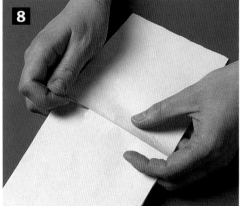

4 Cut a cover from card stock, measuring 11³/₈ in (29 cm) across (11 in [28 cm] + width of spine) and 4¼ in (10½ cm) high. Mark the spine on the cover by making a pencil mark 5½ in (14 cm) from the left and right edges of the cover, at the head of the book. Repeat at the tail. Join the lines vertically. Score along the lines. To cut the buttonhole window, mark a box measuring ³/₄ x 2¹/₈ in (2 x 5½ cm) in the center of the cover. Cut out the box using a craft knife and steel ruler.

7 The holes should be as shown.

8 Pierce the holes in each section as marked using a bookbinder's needle.

5 Fold the cover along the two score lines.

6 Remove the clip from the text block and place the block inside the folded cover. Mark the binding holes by running a pencil along the outside edge of the buttonhole opening.

9 Thread the needle with embroidery thread. Begin sewing by placing the threaded needle into hole No.2 from the inside of just one section. Pull the thread through the outer spine, leaving 2 in (5 cm) of thread inside the section.

10 Place this section into the cover and loop the thread through the buttonhole of the cover.

13 Enter hole No.2 of the next section.

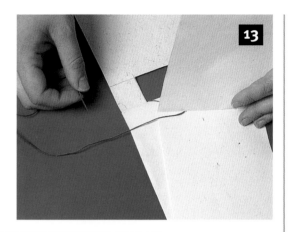

11 Bring the thread-end around the tail of the book. Place the cover and section flat on the work surface and tie a double knot.

14 Loop the thread around the buttonhole cover. Then loop the thread through the stitch of the first section.

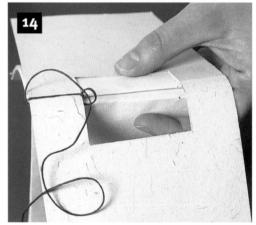

12 Exit through hole No.2 and pull the thread taut.

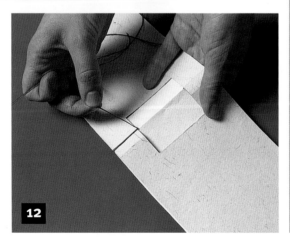

15 Enter hole No.2 of the third section. Continue looping and adding sections in the same manner until all the sections have been added.

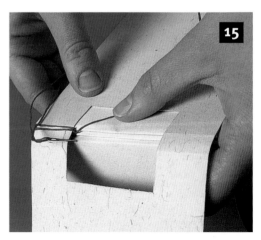

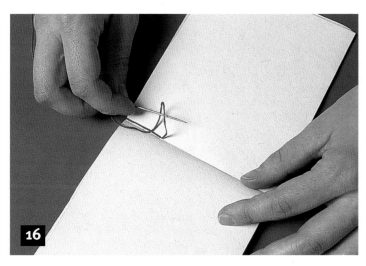

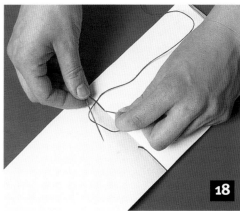

16 On the last section, loop the thread around the tail and tie a double knot flush with the hole. Trim, leaving a ½ in (1½ cm) tail.

17 Repeat steps 10 to 16, sewing hole No.1 and looping the thread around the head of the book.

18 Tie off the thread as in step 16.

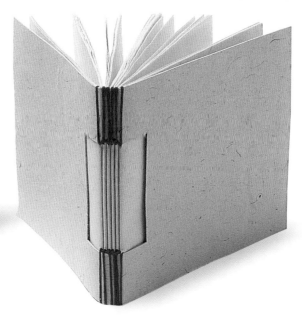

◀ The exposed stitch of the buttonhole stitch binding method gives a book greater flexibility. Flaps can be incorporated at the edges of the cover and folded.

Concertina Binding

The concertina binding technique is one of the most popular binding methods and is widely used by bookbinders because of its flexibility and interesting appearance.

YOU WILL NEED
- sheet of paper, 5 x 7¾ in (12½ x 19½ cm)
- bone folder
- scrap paper
- pencil
- ruler
- 3 sheets of handmade paper, 5½ x 7¾ in (14 x 19½ cm)
- bookbinder's needle
- embroidery thread
- scissors

Concertina binding produces a book where the sections lay flat when opened. Concertina folds may be made wide or narrow, and the number of peaks and valleys may vary. This example shows three single-sheet sections sewn onto three concertina peaks. Select a strong paper for the concertina folds; here, we are using a green-pigmented abaca paper, with deckled edges removed.

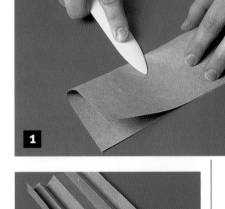

1 Fold a sheet of paper 5 x 7¾ in (12½ x 19½ cm) in half lengthwise. Use a bone folder for a crisp fold.

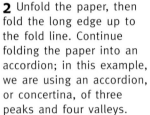

2 Unfold the paper, then fold the long edge up to the fold line. Continue folding the paper into an accordion; in this example, we are using an accordion, or concertina, of three peaks and four valleys.

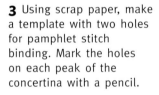

3 Using scrap paper, make a template with two holes for pamphlet stitch binding. Mark the holes on each peak of the concertina with a pencil.

4 Fold three 5½ x 7¾ in (14 x 19½ cm) sheets into single pamphlets. The sheets and concertina should be the same length. Use the template to mark the holes on the single-sheet pamphlets.

5 Pierce the holes in the pamphlets and the concertina with a bookbinder's needle; they should each be 2 in (5 cm) from the head and tail.

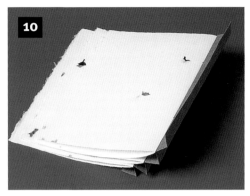

6 Thread the needle with embroidery thread. Attach the pamphlets to the concertina by pulling the thread through the pamphlet from the inside, exiting the pamphlet, and then threading through the first peak of the concertina.

10 The pamphlets are now bound to the concertina, ready for a cover to be applied to the outer fold of the concertina.

7 Pull the thread through the second hole on the peak of the concertina. Thread through the corresponding hole of the pamphlet.

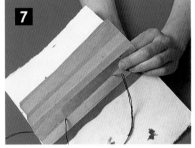

▼ ▶ With concertina binding, the possibilities are endless. You can sew or glue the pages of your book to the folds, dividing individual pages for added variation and interest.

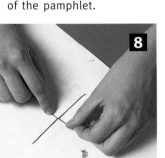

8 Tie a double knot in the inside and center of the pamphlet. Trim the thread to ½ in (1½ cm).

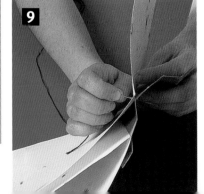

9 Repeat steps 6 to 8 on the remaining pamphlets, attaching a pamphlet to each concertina peak.

Compound Hinging

The flexibility of compound hinging allows pages to open and turn with ease because of the double hinging of the sections and the folds of the pleat. When working with folios, the compound feature allows pages of any thickness to lie flat in an open position.

YOU WILL NEED
- sheet of paper, 5¼ x 11 in (13 x 28 cm)
- bone folder
- scrap paper
- pencil
- ruler
- bookbinder's needle
- 4 sheets of handmade paper, 5½ x 8½ in (14 x 21 cm)
- 2 sheets of handmade paper, 8½ x 11 in (21 x 28 cm)
- embroidery thread

Use a variety of stitches along the concertina spine—pamphlet stitches, fold pages, stab binding, or whatever you prefer.

1 Fold a sheet of paper 5¼ x 11 in (13 x 28 cm) into a concertina with two peaks and one valley. Use a bone folder for a sharp crease.

2 Make a template from scrap paper and mark three holes for a pamphlet stitch on each peak and valley. Pierce the holes with a bookbinder's needle.

3 Fold one set of four sheets, measuring 5½ x 8½ in (14 x 21 cm) unfolded, in half to create a section of eight folios.

4 Create a double-folded section by folding an 8½ x 11 in (21 x 28 cm) sheet of paper in half, and then in quarters. Repeat to make a second section.

5 Use the template to mark the holes for three-hole pamphlet stitch in the center of one double-folded section, placing the holes 2 in (5 cm) from the head and tail, and in the center.

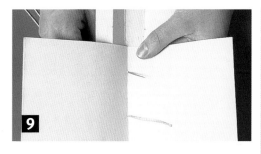

6 Thread the bookbinder's needle with embroidery thread. Attach the first double-folded section to one of the peaks of the concertina by entering the center hole of the section and threading through the center hole on the concertina. Pull the thread through and enter the hole at the head of the concertina. Pull the thread through the concertina and pamphlet, pulling the thread taut.

9 Repeat steps 5 to 8 with the small single-folded section of papers, sewing this section to the valley of the concertina.

7 Enter the center hole, and pull the needle through to the outside of the concertina.

10 Tie the thread using a double knot, placed flush with the center hole. Repeat steps 5 to 8 for the remaining double-folded section, attaching it to the other peak of the concertina.

8 Pull the thread through the hole at the tail of the concertina, and tie off the thread with a double knot flush with the center hole.

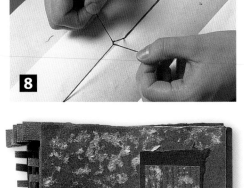

▶ This book was made using compound hinging paired with intricate spinework.

TIP *Vary paper sizes and textures to create interest and appeal.*

DECORATING AND EMBELLISHING

Decorative Coverwork

Decorating your handbound book makes it a unique work of art. Some decorative techniques must be decided upon before constructing the book (such as interlocking tabs, hidden ribbon ties, or spine embellishments). Others can be added once the book is completed (for example, decorations on the cover, or spinework which uses the sewn spine as a foundation).

Don't be limited by the conventional. Most of all, once you have mastered the basics, enjoy creating books that reflect your imagination and creativity and which will be treasured by those fortunate enough to receive one.

YOU WILL NEED
- decorative paper for cover
- craft knife
- cutting mat
- fabric paints
- glitter pen
- stencil
- acrylic stencil paints
- scrap paper
- sponge
- papercast molds
- white glue
- paper pulp

DECORATIVE CUTOUTS

1 Cutout windows are a great way to show off text or images on the inside of the book. This example shows how to create a window in a softcover book. Windows can also be added to hardcover books simply by cutting the window in the book board before it is covered. When the board is covered, cut diagonal slits in the paper that covers the window cutout and wrap the paper around the edges (see Scrapbook, page 126).

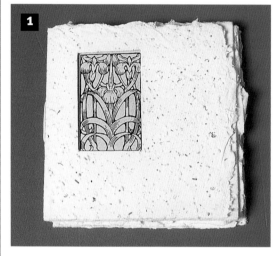

2 Measure and cut a window using a craft knife, working on a cutting mat to protect your work surface.

PAINTS

1 Use fabric paints to embellish a cover. Here, gold glitter and blue fabric paint are used to add squiggles and dots.

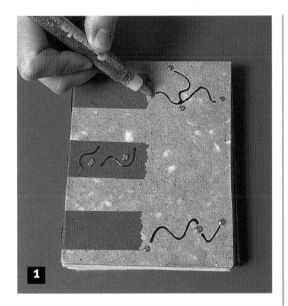

2 Place the stencil on the book cover and gently dab the sponge over the image.

3 Build up layers of paint by continuing to work lightly on the stencil. Add more paint to the sponge as needed.

STENCILING

1 Stencils add interesting detail to a cover. Select a stencil and acrylic stencil paints. Place a dollop of paint on a piece of scrap paper and dab a sponge into the paint. Dab the sponge on a blank area of the paper to work the paint into the sponge, and to eliminate excess paint.

▼ The finished piece features a golden fall leaf.

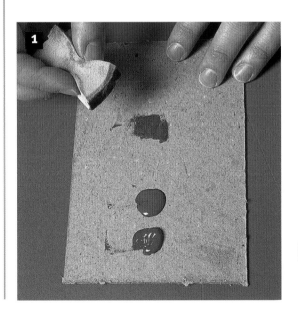

PAPERCASTING

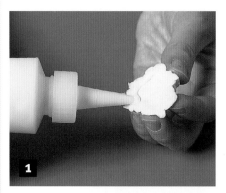

1 Using the papercasting techniques shown on pages 42–43 to make a papercast to feature on the cover of a book. Place a thin layer of white glue on the back of the papercast.

2 Place the papercast on the cover of a book.

YOU WILL NEED
- colored ink
- rubber stamp
- paper for front cover
- glitter pen
- beads
- raffia
- scissors

STAMPING

1 Stamping is a great way to produce multiples of an image. Colored inks, embossing powders, and fine tipped pens, all supplies from rubber stamping crafts, may be used to embellish the cover. Apply ink to the stamp. Here we are using a roller ink for re-inking stamp pads.

2 Stamp the image on the cover of the book by placing the image on paper and pressing with firm and even pressure.

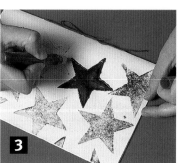

3 Apply glitter detail by outlining the star with a glitter pen. A contrasting glitter color adds extra interest.

BEADS

1 Use beads for decorating a cover by threading them onto the front binding. Pull raffia through the binding holes of the book. Thread beads onto the raffia.

2 Tie the ends of the raffia securely.

3 Tie the raffia ends into a bow and trim neatly to finish.

▲ ▶ Decorative coverwork can take so many different forms. You can add splash and color to a cover (above), use a star punch around the sides (right), or add beads and raffia to create a strong finishing touch.

Decorative Spinework

Using wires, ribbons, and beads, it is possible to add something that will enhance the appearance of a handbound book and add meaning to the overall effect. A tiny seashell suspended from a thread could grace the spine of a holiday journal.

Beads from a favorite piece of jewelry find new life on the spine of a beautiful book. Try different ideas to give your books added personality and flair.

YOU WILL NEED
- bookbinder's needle
- handbound book
- medium-gauge wire
- snug-nosed pliers
- pamphlet-stitch book
- binding thread
- ornament
- ribbon

WIRE BINDING

1 Pierce holes in the text block and book cover with a bookbinder's needle, and cut a length of medium-gauge wire. Insert the wire by hand or by using snug-nosed pliers. Thread both ends of the wire from the back to the front of the book.

2 Using the snug-nosed pliers, bend the wire so that it lies flat on the front cover of the book.

3 Thread the wire ends back into the holes and through to the back.

4 Loop the wire ends around each other to secure. Use pliers to tuck in the ends.

TIP *Gold and silver tone wire is often available in the jewelry supply section of a craft store.*

ALTERNATIVE WIRE BINDING

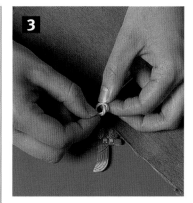

1 Instead of tucking in the wire ends, use snug-nosed pliers to bend the wire into squiggly shapes.

HANGING DECORATION

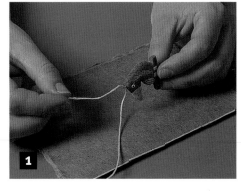

1 Design and prepare a pamphlet-stitch book. Select binding thread in the same or a complementary color. Thread a bookbinder's needle with the binding thread and pull it through the top hole of the binding. Leave one end of the thread inside the book and pull the other end through completely. Thread the ornament, in this case a wooden parrot, onto the binding thread.

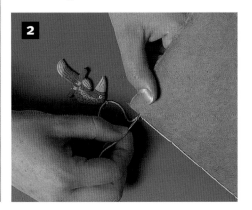

2 Pull the needle and thread back through the top hole.

3 Tie a double knot on the inside of the pamphlet.

4 Allow the ornament to hang from the spine.

RIBBON BINDING

Use a beautiful ribbon to bind a stab-bound book. End the sewing with the ribbon tails on the front of the book, and tie the ends into a pretty bow.

Tabs and Ties

Creative closures on handmade books serve two purposes—that of adding a personal, decorative touch to the book, and of protecting the inside pages.

INTERLOCKING FLAP

1 Using a bone folder, make a fold in a 6 x 9 in (15 x 23 cm) sheet of paper, folding on the 9 in (23 cm) length and leaving a flap 2½ in (6 cm) long. Fold this flap to crease, then open it to prepare for marking and trimming.

YOU WILL NEED
- bone folder
- sheet of paper, 6 x 9 in (15 x 23 cm)
- steel ruler
- craft knife
- cutting mat
- pencil
- decorative cord or raffia
- small piece of paper
- white glue
- corrugated card cover for fold book
- brayer (small roller)
- brick wrapped in paper as a weight

2 Mark the center point along the side of the flap.

3 Using a steel ruler and craft knife, and working on a cutting mat to protect the work surface, cut diagonally from the center point to the flap fold. Repeat on the other side of the flap to create a pointed flap.

4 Fold the flap in and smooth with a bone folder.

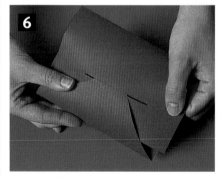

5 To create a slot for the flap, measure 1½ in (4 cm) in from the flap fold. Use a pencil to mark either side of the flap. Open up the cover and connect the two points with a pencil and ruler. Cut the slot with a craft knife to ¹⁄₁₆ in (1 mm).

6 Slip the flap into the slot to complete.

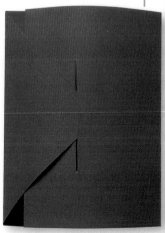

INTERLOCKING TAB

1

Try this variation for a different tab look.

1 Create a tab from the flap shown in step 1 (page opposite). Cut a tab centered on the flap, measuring 1 in (2½ cm) wide and 3 in (7½ cm) long.

2 Cut the slot, as shown in step 5 (page opposite), by measuring on either side of the tab and cutting a slot of ⅟₁₆ in (1 mm).

2

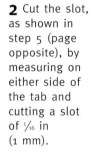

TIES

1 Prepare a fold book, as shown on pages 92–93. Cut a length of decorative cord, and place it on the front of the fold book, at the center of the foredge. Cut a small piece of paper and glue it over the cord with white glue to hold it in place.

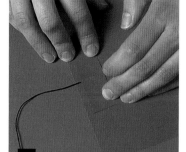

1

2 Using white glue, glue a cover onto the outside of the fold book, thereby covering up the glued tie.

3

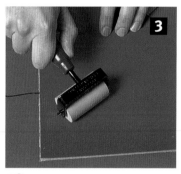

2

3 Turn the book over and use a brayer to roll the paper onto the corrugated cover. Place it under a weight until dry.

◀ You can use raffia to tie your book (left) as an alternative to decorative cord.

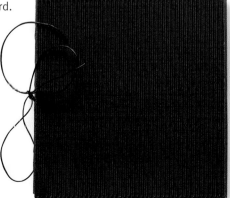

PROJECTS
Single-section Notebook

For someone new to bookbinding, this is a good book with which to begin. The single section makes a fine little book as it is, or it may be given added covering and decorative touches (see pages 110–117).

YOU WILL NEED
- 8 sheets of cotton and petals handmade paper, 8½ x 11 in (21 x 28 cm)
- bone folder
- medium-weight white vellum, 8½ x 11 in (21 x 28 cm)
- craft knife, steel ruler, and cutting mat
- medium-weight sage paper, 9 x 12 in (23 x 30 cm)
- pencil and clips
- awl and hammer
- 3 strands of green embroidery thread, 18 in (45 cm) long
- bookbinder's needle
- scissors
- sheet of rust paper, cut to 4½ x 7 in (11 x 18 cm)
- white glue
- preserved leaf

1 Select eight sheets of 8½ x 11 in (21 x 28 cm) cotton and petals paper. Jog the stack together. Fold the stack in half using a bone folder.

2 Create a flyleaf by folding one sheet of 8½ x 11 in (21 x 28 cm) vellum in half. Slip the cotton and petals section into the flyleaf to prepare for binding.

3 Using a craft knife and steel ruler, and working on a cutting mat to protect the work surface, cut a cover of medium-weight sage paper, measuring 9 x 12 in (23 x 30 cm).

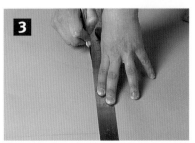

4 Fold the cover in half, and crease the fold with a bone folder. Place the section, together with the vellum flyleaf, into the cover.

5 Use clips to clamp the cover to the section. Using a ruler and pencil, mark two holes 1¾ in (4½ cm) from the head and tail of the book. Mark a center hole with a pencil.

TIP *If the clips make creases in the paper, fold a scrap of paper and place it between the clip and the book, to protect the book.*

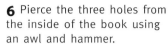

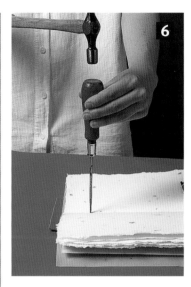

6 Pierce the three holes from the inside of the book using an awl and hammer.

7 Using three strands of green embroidery thread, thread a bookbinder's needle. Begin sewing by entering the center hole from the outside of the book. Pull the thread through, leaving 4 in (10 cm) of thread on the outside of the book.

8 Enter the bottom hole and pull the thread through to the outside of the book. Enter the center hole, and pull the thread to the inside. Enter the top hole and pull the thread through. Ensure that the thread is taut all along the spine.

9 On the exterior of the spine, tie a double knot. Trim the threads to equal lengths.

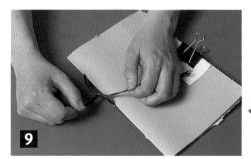

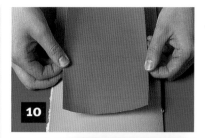

10 Cut a piece of contrasting paper to 4½ in (11 cm) wide by 7 in (18 cm) long. Here, we used a rust-colored paper stock. Glue this to the front of the book cover.

11 Apply a thin layer of white glue to a preserved leaf.

12 Position the leaf in the center of the rust paper, pointing from corner to corner. Gently smooth in place.

▼ You can use this notebook to record your special gardening tips and projects.

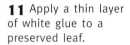

Pocket-sized Travel Journal

This book follows the same steps as the sample book on pages 94–96. The sample book shows how to make a template for piercing holes; here, we show you how to measure the holes without a template. Use the technique that you prefer.

YOU WILL NEED

- 2 pieces of book board, 4½ x 5½ in (11 x 14 cm)
- 2 sheets of handmade tea paper, 6½ x 7½ in (16½ x 19 cm)
- wheat paste
- small brush
- 2 sheets of handmade tea paper, 4⅛ x 5¼ in (10 x 13 cm)
- brayer (small roller)
- brick wrapped in paper, as a weight
- 35 sheets of letter-weight medium brown paper, 5½ x 8½ in (14 x 21 cm)
- bone folder
- clip
- 2 pieces of ribbon, 1⅜ in (3½ cm) wide, 12 in (30 cm) long
- pencil
- bookbinder's needle
- 2 pieces of black waxed linen cord, 30 in (75 cm) long
- scissors
- white glue
- piece of brown leather, 2¾ x 5½ in (7 x 14 cm)
- spatula
- 2 glassine envelopes, 3¾ x 4½ in (9½ x 11 cm)

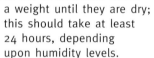

1 Using the hardcover techniques (see pages 84–87), cover each book board with 6½ x 7½ in (16½ x 19 cm) tea paper. Unlike the example on page 84, these boards do not have a hinge. Apply a sheet of 4⅛ x 5¼ in (10 x 13 cm) tea paper to the back of the book boards, and use the brayer to smooth the paper evenly. Place the book covers under a weight until they are dry; this should take at least 24 hours, depending upon humidity levels.

2 Prepare the text block by counting 35 sheets of medium brown paper into seven stacks of five sheets each. Using a bone folder, fold each stack in half. Print lines on the pages or leave blank, as desired.

3 Place the sections in a stack and put under a weight for three to four hours. Remove the weight and secure at the head with a clip. Place a length of ribbon 1 in (2½ cm) from the tail of the stack, and with a pencil, mark on either side, running the pencil up and down the stack to mark each section. Repeat with a ribbon at the head of the book.

TIP *If the covers do not dry within 24 to 48 hours, use a fan to blow air on the stack. In areas of high humidity, place the covers between paper blotters, and leave under a weight. Change the blotters as often as needed, to ensure that the covers do not begin to mildew.*

4 Remove the clip from the sections and pierce holes at each marking. Each section will have four holes, two on either side of where the ribbons will be placed.

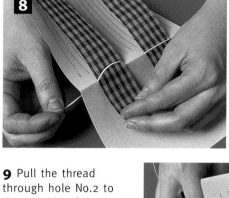

8 Enter hole No.2 from the inside, then exit, and enter hole No.1. Place the second ribbon within the loop and pull the thread taut.

5 Thread a bookbinder's needle with linen cord. Begin sewing in the first section by entering hole No.3. Pull the needle and thread to the outside. Leave a tail of thread 5 in (12½ cm) long inside the section, and enter hole No.4.

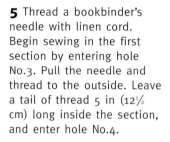

6 Place the ribbon in the loop of thread, and pull the thread taut to hold the ribbon in place.

9 Pull the thread through hole No.2 to the outside of the section. Enter hole No.2 of the next section and pull the thread to the inside. Enter hole No.1, pulling the thread to the outside, and enter hole No.2 again. Slip the ribbon into the loop of thread, placing this second section in place on the first section. Pull the thread taut and enter hole No.3. Continue sewing in this manner until all sections have been added. (See page 94 for detailed instructions on sewing technique with tapes.)

7 Tie a double knot in the inside of the section.

10 In the last section, tie a double knot on the inside of the section.

TIP *When you run out of binding thread midway through the project, add on a second strand at the inside of a section. Stop binding at hole No.2 or No.3, leaving at least 2 in (5 cm) of thread. With the second thread, tie a knot at the base of the finished thread. Push the knot to be flush with the book section. Thread the needle with the second thread and continue binding. Trim the knot when you have finished binding.*

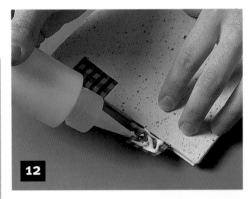

12 Apply a thin layer of white glue to the front of the ribbons. Be careful not to get glue on the pages.

13 Place a cover on top of the text block and smooth the ribbons in place. The line of the ribbons should be parallel to the head and tail of the book cover. Repeat with the back cover.

11 Trim the ribbons to 1½ in (4 cm) on the front and back of the book.

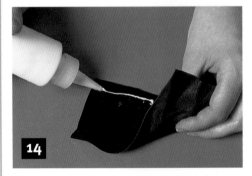

14 Apply a thin, even layer of white glue to the piece of leather.

15 Position the leather on the spine of the book, tugging gently to wrap it evenly around the front and back of the book.

16 Apply a thin layer of white glue to the first page of the book.

17 Smooth the glue evenly over the page with a spatula.

18 Smooth the page down onto the cover using a brayer. This technique secures the cover to the text block. Repeat with the other cover.

19 Apply a thin layer of white glue to a glassine envelope.

20 Position the envelope in the center of the inside front cover and smooth with a brayer. Repeat with a second glassine envelope on the inside back cover.

▼ A small-sized hardcover journal like this is perfect for keeping a record of your travel or vacation memories.

TIP *Adhesive will seep through some parts of the ribbons. Gently wipe away excess glue and let dry. Most white glues will dry clear and matte.*

Scrapbook

A window on the front cover may be used to hold a favorite photo or drawing to set the theme for your memory album. The use of spacers will allow you to add photographs, clippings, and special memories to the pages of this book.

YOU WILL NEED

- wheat paste
- small brush
- 2 sheets of handmade moss and petals paper, 14 x 17 in (35 x 43 cm)
- 2 pieces of book board, 12 x 12 in (30 x 30 cm)
- 2 sheets of yellow machine-made paper, 10 x 11¼ in (25 x 28 cm)
- white glue
- brayer (small roller)
- brick wrapped in paper, as a weight
- 10 sheets of white machine-made paper, 11¾ x 13½ in (29½ x 33 cm)
- ruler
- pencil
- bone folder
- 2 clamps
- sheet of paper for template for binding holes
- hammer
- awl
- bookbinder's needle
- piece of tan leather cord, 40 in (100 cm) long
- twig
- piece of cardboard, 5½ x 7 in (14 x 18 cm)
- craft knife
- steel ruler
- cutting mat
- sheet of handmade moss and petals paper, 8½ x 11 in (21 x 28 cm)

1 Paste a sheet of 14 x 17 in (35 x 43 cm) moss and petals paper to the back cover book board. Repeat with the front cover book board, taking special care to miter the corners. (See pages 84–87 for detailed instructions on pasting and mitering.)

2 Apply a sheet of yellow machine-made paper to the inside of each cover using white glue. Roll in place using a brayer. Place both covers under a weight for 24 to 48 hours or until dry.

3 Create a spacer between each inner page by folding a 1½ in (3½ cm) flap on each sheet. Use a ruler and pencil to mark 1½ in (3½ cm) from the edge, and make a crease with a bone folder. The folded page should now measure 11¾ x 11¾ in (29½ x 29½ cm).

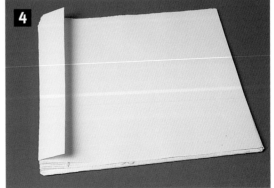

4 Repeat with each page.

5 To assemble the book covers and pages, first place the back cover down, with the yellow paper side facing upward. Place the stack of book pages on the back cover, each with the flap on the left side, folded face up. Finally, place the front cover on top of the stack, with the moss and petals side facing upward, and with the hinge on the lefthand side. Secure the book with a clamp at both the head and tail of the book.

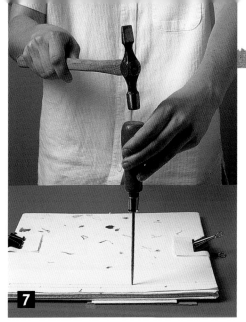

7 Using a hammer and awl, pierce the holes through the covers and text block.

6 Create a paper template for binding holes by marking the following: a) four holes 1 in (2½ cm) from the spine, and 1 in (2½ cm) from the head and tail, with 3¼ in (8 cm) between each hole; and b) three holes ⅝ in (2 cm) from the spine, and 2⅝ in (6 cm) from the head and tail, with 3¼ in (8 cm) between each hole.

8 Thread a bookbinder's needle with leather cord. Begin sewing at the back of the book using the sewing route described on pages 100–101. At the third hole from the top, place the twig in place and sew over it to secure in place.

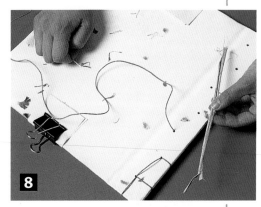

9 Continue sewing down the spine of the book. Sew up to the top of the book and tie the cords off when you reach the top hole. (See pages 100–101 for detailed instructions.) Put the book aside.

TIP It is often a good idea to add spacers to a scrapbook, when it will be filled with bulky materials. The added space between each sheet reduces bulging by making room for added thickness.

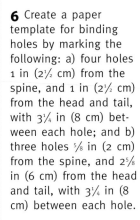

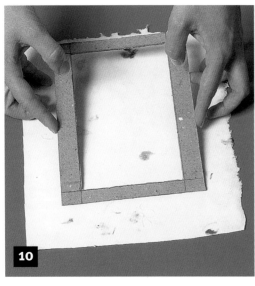

10 To create a frame for the cover of the book, cut a rectangle measuring 4½ x 5½ in (11 x 14 cm) from the center of the cardboard.

Work on a cutting mat to protect the work surface. The remaining frame should measure 5½ x 7 in (14 x 18 cm) with the top and bottom sides of the frame ¾ in (2 cm) wide and the left and right sides of the frame 1 in (2½ cm) wide. Apply wheat paste to the frame and place it on an 8½ x 11 in (21 x 28 cm) sheet of handmade moss and petals paper.

11 Turn the frame over and use a brayer to smooth it.

12 Using a steel ruler and craft knife, cut two diagonal slits, creating four triangles of paper in the center of the frame.

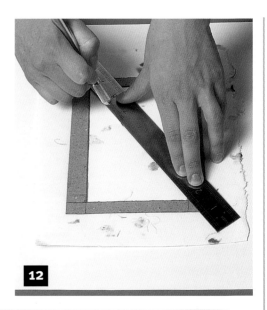

13 Fold the paper outward over the frame and fix in place using wheat paste.

14 Trim the excess paper, leaving a 1 in (2½ cm) flap along each side.

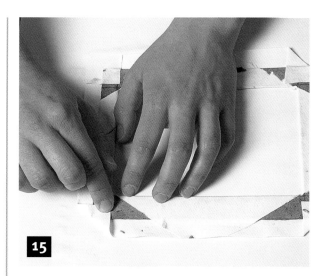

15

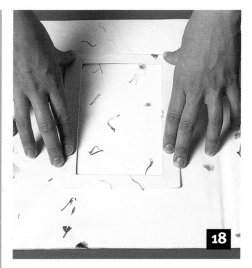

18 Place the frame, glue side down, centered on the cover of the book and positioned with the unglued edge at the head of the book.

18

15 Miter the corners and paste in place (see page 86).

16 Paste the edges and smooth in place.

16

▼ You can add the final touches to your scrapbook cover with colorful handmade paper and mementos of vacations gone by.

17 Apply a thin layer of white glue to the bottom, left, and right edges of the frame. Leave the top edge unglued to allow a picture to be slipped into the frame.

17

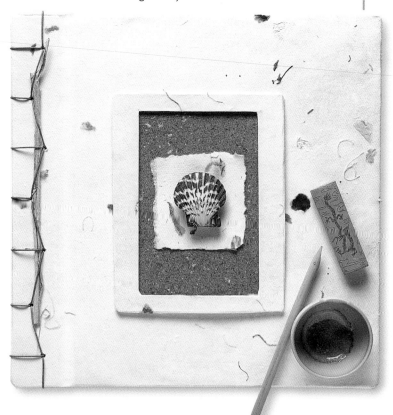

Baby Brag Book

Here is a special journal for recording those thoughts and treasured moments so that one day you can give it to your grown-up child. The unique tab closure ensures protection for the pages inside and a degree of privacy for the writer! Embellish the cover with a papercast object to personalize the book.

YOU WILL NEED
- 7 sheets of white machine-made paper, 6 x 16½ in (15 x 42 cm)
- bone folder
- sheet of purple machine-made card stock, 6 x 20 in (15 x 50 cm)
- pencil
- ruler
- steel ruler
- craft knife
- bookbinder's needle
- waxed purple embroidery thread, 5 ft (1½ m) long
- white glue
- papercast butterfly
- set of Velcro tabs

1 Fold a sheet of white machine-made paper in half widthwise, using a bone folder for a sharp crease. Open out the sheet and fold it into quarters by bringing each end to meet in the center. Fold the sheet in half and put it aside. Fold the remaining sheets in the same manner.

2 Take one folded sheet and place it on top of a sheet of purple machine-made card stock, flush with the left side of the card stock. Mark the right side of the sheet on the purple card stock with a pencil.

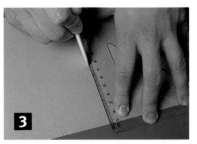

3 Make 14 additional marks to the right of this marking, on the card stock, each ⅜ in (8 mm) apart, at the head and tail of the cover. With a ruler and bone folder, score the cover along the 15 marked points.

4 Carefully fold the card stock at the marks, alternating folding in and out to create the concertina folds of the cover.

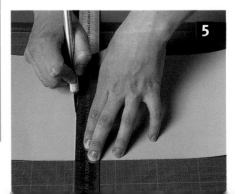

5 Measure off 4 in (10 cm) from the back cover using a steel ruler and craft knife.

6 On the back cover piece, mark a straight line in pencil to define the back cover, 4⅛ in (10 cm) from the last fold of the concertina, and drawn from head to tail of the cover. On this line, measure and mark a point 2½ in (6 cm) from the head and another point 2½ in (6 cm) from the tail. Make the same two marks on the other edge of the back cover. Connect the points to form a tab, and trim using a steel ruler and craft knife.

7 On each folded inner page, mark two holes, 2 in (5 cm) apart, and 2 in (5 cm) from the head and tail. Pierce the holes with a bookbinder's needle. Make the same markings on the valleys of the concertina folds, and pierce with a bookbinder's needle.

8 Sew each folded page onto a concertina valley using the two-hole pamphlet stitch.

TIP The concertina folds consist of peaks and valleys. You may bind your book on either the peak or the valley, depending upon the look desired. This project binds the pages on the valley. Try binding on the peak, but be sure to enlarge the front and back covers to accommodate the change.

9 Tie a double knot on the inside of each page.

10 Apply a thin layer of white glue to the back of the papercast butterfly. Press the butterfly firmly onto the cover, and place it under a light weight for 30 minutes.

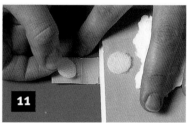

11 Trim the tab to 1½ in (3½ cm). Fold it over to the front cover. Attach one half of a tab of Velcro to the cover and one half to the card tab.

▶ Make this book for a friend to record her new baby's first year. Personalize the cover with a papercast embellishment or a photograph mounted on deckle-edged handmade paper.

Buttonhole Book

A little careful measuring and cutting is worth the effort to produce this delightful book with the surprise binding feature. This is sure to become a favorite of yours and a coveted gift for a friend.

YOU WILL NEED

- 72 sheets of cream paper, 4¼ x 8½ in (10½ x 21 cm)
- bone folder
- brick wrapped in paper, as a weight
- clip
- craft knife
- steel ruler
- cutting mat
- sheet of purple card stock, 4¼ x 9 in (10½ x 23 cm)
- pencil
- bookbinder's needle
- waxed white embroidery thread
- white acrylic paint
- rubber star stamp
- sponge

1 Sort the sheets of cream paper into nine sets of eight sheets each. Jog the edge of one set, and fold it in half using a bone folder. Repeat with the remaining sets. Position the sections in a stack and place under a weight for three to four hours. Clip the sections together; trim the foredge using a craft knife and a steel ruler.

2 Using the technique described on page 102, mark a ½ in (1½ cm) spine in the center of the purple card stock. Mark and cut out a box in the center of the cover, measuring 2 in (5 cm) wide and 3 in (7½ cm) high. This box will form the buttonhole of the book cover.

3 Score the spine and fold it into the cover.

4 Remove the sections from under the weight and place them inside the cover. Using a pencil, mark the edge of the buttonhole on the sections.

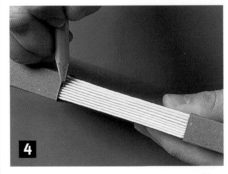

5 Remove the sections from the book cover and pierce the holes where marked with a bookbinder's needle.

6 Thread a bookbinder's needle with waxed embroidery thread. Enter the hole at the tail of the book from inside and pull the thread to the outside. Leave 2 in (5 cm) of thread inside the book. Wrap the thread around the tail of the buttonhole cover and tie the thread with the end inside the book. Tie a double knot over the hole.

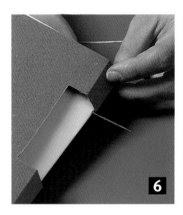

7 Exit the hole at the tail of the book, and add a second section by entering the same hole of the next section.

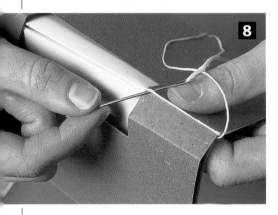

8 Loop the thread around the tail of the buttonhole cover and link it into the thread of the first section. Continue adding sections in the same manner until they have all been added.

9 Sew the sections to the head of the book by following steps 6 to 8.

10 Apply white acrylic paint to a rubber star stamp with a sponge, then stamp a white star on the front cover. Lift up the stamp carefully to reveal the image.

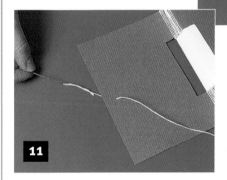

11 Pierce a hole in the center edge of the front and back covers, and thread two pieces of white embroidery thread through both holes. Tie the threads together in a bow for a decorative closure.

▼ Experiment with different colors of card stock and vary the cover image to make unique creations to delight family and friends.

Hardcover Portfolio

Use this unique portfolio to present or store important documents or manuscripts. The tidy pockets will ensure the safety of the papers and the beautiful papers chosen will reflect your personal style.

YOU WILL NEED
- small brush
- wheat paste
- 2 sheets of gold paper, 10 x 13 in (25 x 32½ cm)
- 2 pieces of book board, 8½ x 11 in (21 x 28 cm)
- brayer (small roller)
- sheet of sage green paper, 22 x 30 in (55 x 75 cm)
- craft knife
- steel ruler
- cutting mat
- white glue
- spatula

1 Using a small brush, apply wheat paste to the reverse side of a piece of gold paper, then place a book board in the center of the gold paper. Using a brayer, roll the paper smooth on the gold side.

2 Miter the corners of the paper and fold in the edges, using the technique described on page 86. Repeat with the second board and sheet of gold paper.

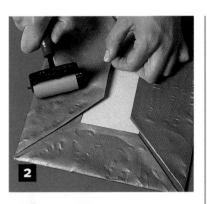

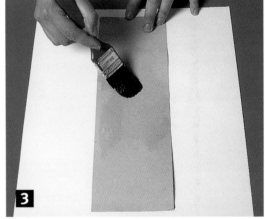

3 Cut a strip of sage green paper, 2½ in (6 cm) wide and 13 in (32½ cm) long. Apply paste to one side of the paper.

4 Center the covered boards on the strip of sage green paper, leaving a center gutter equal to the thickness of both boards.

TIP *Leave a gutter equal to the thickness of the two boards, when placed one of top of the other, in order to be able to fold and close the portfolio.*

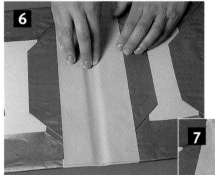

5 Apply a small amount of white glue to the flap of green paper at the top and bottom and fold the flaps around the edge of the boards. Smooth the green paper with your fingers.

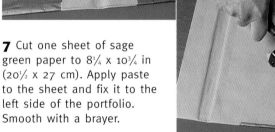

6 Cut a strip of sage green paper to 2½ in (6 cm) wide and 10½ in (27½ cm) long. Paste and apply to the inner spine of the portfolio.

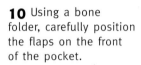

7 Cut one sheet of sage green paper to 8¼ x 10¾ in (20½ x 27 cm). Apply paste to the sheet and fix it to the left side of the portfolio. Smooth with a brayer.

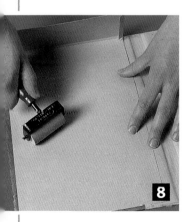

8 Trim a sheet of sage green paper to the dimensions shown right. Score and fold the pocket across the dotted line. Apply paste to the back of the pocket. Smooth in place on the portfolio's back cover with a brayer.

9 Apply white glue to the flap of the pocket.

10 Using a bone folder, carefully position the flaps on the front of the pocket.

▶ The use of gold and sage green lends the portfolio an air of elegant formality.

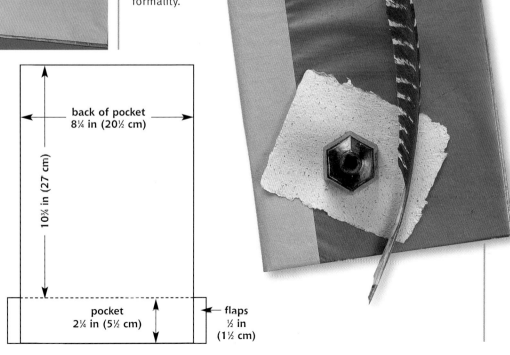

back of pocket
8¼ in (20½ cm)

10¾ in (27 cm)

pocket
2¼ in (5½ cm)

flaps
½ in
(1½ cm)

Post and Screw Photo Album

This album is both beautiful and practical. Pages may easily be added or removed because of the post and screw binding. The raffia tie closure is an attractive design feature and complements the grass paper used for the cover.

YOU WILL NEED
- sheet of book board, 5½ x 7½ in (14 x 19 cm)
- sheet of book board, 5½ x 6 in (14 x 15 cm)
- 2 sheets of handmade prairie grass paper, 8½ x 11 in (21 x 28 cm)
- wheat paste
- small brush
- white glue
- 2 lengths of raffia
- 2 sheets of handmade prairie grass paper, 5 x 7 in (12½ x 18 cm)
- brick wrapped in paper, as a weight
- 2 sheets of white medium-weight vellum
- 15 sheets of handmade classic cotton paper, 5 x 7 in (12½ x 18 cm)
- clips
- sheet of book board, 1 x 5½ in (2½ x 14 cm) for template
- hammer
- awl
- 2 posts and screws
- screwdriver

1 Paste and cover the front and back boards with handmade prairie grass paper (see the steps on pages 84–87).

2 Cut or tear a small piece of prairie grass paper to approximately 2 x 3 in (5 x 7½ cm). Apply a layer of white glue over the paper. Position a strip of raffia at the foredge of the book, and cover the end with pasted prairie grass paper. Repeat with the back cover.

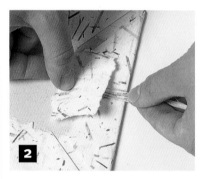

3 Paste and apply a sheet of 5 x 7 in (12½ x 18 cm) prairie grass paper to the inside of the front cover. Repeat with the back cover. Place the cover under a weight to dry.

4 Cut two sheets of vellum measuring 5 x 7 in (12½ x 18 cm).

5 Place a sheet of vellum on either side of the stack of classic cotton paper. Place the stack between the book covers and secure with clips.

6 Create a template for the two holes, ¾ in (2 cm) in from the edge of the spine and 1½ in (4 cm) from the head and tail. Attach the template to the book spine and pierce the holes using a hammer and awl.

7 Insert the post and screw into each hole. Tighten with a screwdriver.

▶ The raffia tie plays beautifully to the handmade paper cover.

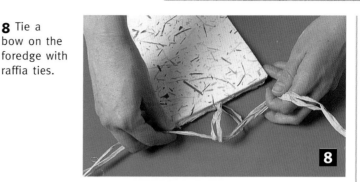

8 Tie a bow on the foredge with raffia ties.

9 Trim the ends to make the bow neater.

Fold Book

The outstanding feature of fold books is that they are made entirely without sewing. Folding creates the structure and must be done carefully in order to make each page the same size. In this book, the marbled pages from the Papermaking section (see pages 40–41) are used as endpapers.

YOU WILL NEED

- bone folder
- sheet of lightweight poster board, 22 x 30 in (55 x 75 cm)
- craft knife
- steel ruler
- cutting mat
- sheet of marbled paper, 8½ x 11 in (21 x 28 cm)
- wheat paste
- small brush
- 2 pieces of book board, 3¾ x 5½ in (9½ x 14 cm)
- brayer (small roller)
- brick wrapped in paper, as a weight

1 Using a bone folder, fold a sheet of poster board in half along the long side. Open up the sheet and fold each edge into the center, to fold the sheet into four long strips measuring 7½ x 22 in (19 x 55 cm) each.

2 Fold each strip in half, creating eight long strips measuring 3¾ x 22 in (9½ x 55 cm) each.

3 Open out the sheet and fold the shorter side in half, creating 16 rectangles, each measuring 3¾ x 11 in (9½ x 28 cm). Fold the edge into the center fold line to produce four folds, and 32 rectangles, each measuring 3¾ x 5½ in (9½ x 14 cm).

4 Open out the sheet and smooth it lightly. Using a craft knife and steel ruler, and working on a cutting mat, cut a straight line from point 1 to point 2.

Diagram for steps 4–6

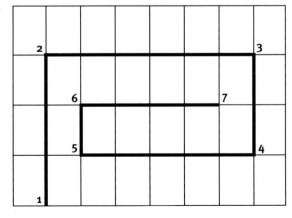

5 Turn the sheet and cut from point 2 to point 3.

6 Turn the sheet and cut from point 3 to point 4. Continue cutting, connecting point 4 to points 5, 6, and 7. The sheet will now be cut into a long snakelike shape. Fold it into a compact fold book, starting at point 1 and folding back and forth to point 7.

7 Cut the sheet of marbled paper in half, to create two book board covers.

8 Apply wheat paste to the book boards and place them on the marbled paper, with the marbled side facing downward.

▶ This book can be used to display pictures, photographs, or sketches, or used as a guest or autograph book.

9 Roll and miter the corners as shown on page 86.

10 Apply paste to the reverse of the front cover.

11 Apply the first page of the folded book onto the pasted front cover. Press firmly and smooth in place with a brayer. Repeat with the back cover. Press under a weight for 24 to 48 hours, or until dry.

CHAPTER 3
Gallery

THE PURPOSE OF THE GALLERY IS TO GIVE THE READER
AN EXPERIENCE OF VIEWING MANY FINE EXAMPLES
OF PAPER AS ART WITHOUT HAVING TO TRAVEL
TO SEVERAL CONTINENTS.

IT WOULD BE IMPOSSIBLE TO PRESENT A THOROUGHLY
REPRESENTATIVE SELECTION OF THE WORKS OF
CONTEMPORARY PAPERMAKERS IN ONE GALLERY SECTION.
IN THIS SELECTION, YOU WILL FIND A VARIETY OF
TECHNIQUE AND DESIGN IDEAS WHICH CAUGHT THE
ATTENTION OF THE AUTHORS. LET THESE WORKS
INSPIRE YOU TO GREATER HEIGHTS IN PAPERMAKING
AND BOOKBINDING.

COMBINE SEVERAL TECHNIQUES TO CREATE NEW
PIECES AND DISCOVER THE INCREDIBLE DIVERSITY OF
PAPER AS A MEDIUM. CONNECT WITH LOCAL
PAPERMAKERS AND BOOKBINDERS TO INSPIRE AND
ENCOURAGE ONE ANOTHER.

Papermaking Gallery

Some of the most wonderful things in life are those surprise moments when you discover the completely unexpected. This is true in papermaking where techniques of papercasting, laminating, and embossing are used alone or in combination to create striking three-dimensional examples of paper art. The pieces in this gallery contain surprise elements which, in combination with handmade paper, form works of beauty and mystery.

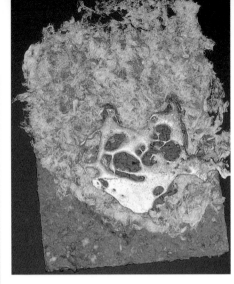

▲ JEAN MARVELL
Discoveries IX
Jean makes use of the foam that appears on the surface of beaten abaca pulp to which has been added methyl cellulose, calcium carbonate, and pigment. The foam forms as the pulp is beaten. The sheets are formed using a shallow dip method and air-drying.

While skimming foam from the surface of her vat, Jean Marvell discovered a unique effect which she has incorporated into her art. In "Discoveries IX," she has combined bronze with this new technique for an amazing textural effect. From Mayka's delicate "Paper Flowers" to the bold color and texture of Marie Wright's "Rothbury Cross Fragment," these pieces reveal the incredible scope and flexibility of the medium of paper in contemporary art.

Many talented paper artists are exploring this medium and developing new techniques while practicing the ancient art and craft of hand papermaking. Here are a few representative pieces of some contemporary artists in the field of paper arts. Each one is combining the old with the new to produce unique results.

ELIZABETH COUZINS-SCOTT ▶
Paper Collage
The rich colors in this piece come from the combination of leaf skeletons and recycled paper pulp. The pulp is beaten and a thin layer is poured over the leaves, allowing the color to show through the pulp layer.

◀ HELMUT FRERICK
Light Pieces
Overbeaten hemp pulp is the base for this piece. The pulp is dyed, cast, and sprayed, and then illuminated from the inside. This piece is part of a full installation, with pieces up to 9 ft (3 m) long.

▼ JEAN MARVELL
Garden Series I–88
This piece uses cotton pulp and a sheet formation technique for making "Plop" or "Puddle" paper. The pigmented paper was sized with Daniel Smith surface sizing and then painted with watercolors.

◀ ROSA DAVIS
Presence
Made from recycled Nepaline paper pulp molded over a form of crumpled paper and packing tape, this piece is embellished with bright silk appliqués.

◀ **MARIE WRIGHT**
Rothbury Cross
Fragment
Handmade cotton
and straw paper with
muslin forms the base
of this work, which also
features an engraved
and screenprinted
monoprint with fine
detail. Driftwood
and leather thongs
frame the top and
bottom edges.

◀ **JANE PRICE**
Cone and Cylinders
A cone and cylinders with
peeling alder bark, hellebore,
and montbretia stems form
the structure for the cast pulp
and machine stitching. The
pulp is made from silk
wastes, alder bark, and
plant material.

◀ **SUZIE BALAZS**
Returning from Market—
Bolivia
Handmade paper from recycled rag-paper offcuts forms the thick base of this piece. Muslin forms the next layer with colored pulp and thread added for texture and detail. Pastel and acrylic paint embellishments, as well as folded and painted Japanese paper, create depth and intricacy.

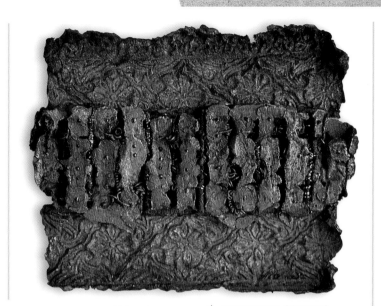

▲ **ELIZABETH COUZINS-SCOTT Nocturne**
Recycled paper is the base pulp used in this work. The pulp has been used with techniques of impressing and casting over found objects and an Indian wooden block.

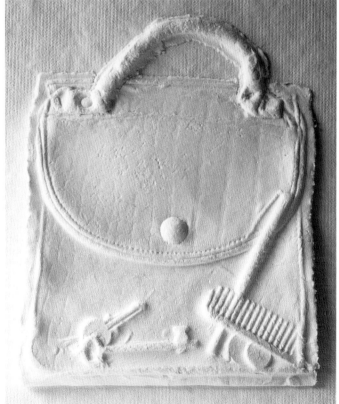

◀ **CAROLE ANDREWS**
Open Sphere
The paper in this piece was made from recycled industrial paper and a technique of "smocking" was used to create the unique texture.

◀ **DIANE READE**
Handbag
Cotton linters formed the base pulp which was cast over a plaster mold for this X-ray type image.

**▼ ▶ MAYKA TORREADRADO
Paper Flowers**
These flowers are made from commercially sold handmade paper (khadi) embroidered with rayon thread using a vintage treadle machine.

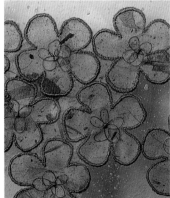

**◀ COCO GORDON
Stolen Hammock**
Made from linen yarn and a hand-woven mold, the yarn is Hollander-beaten to partly produce a flax-like pulp. From a series of eight life-size hammocks.

**DIANE READE ▶
Insects in Jars**
Cotton sheets are cast over a plaster mold and then reformed into cylinders.

◀ **CAROLE ANDREWS**
Interrupted Spheres
These origami figures
are made from
industrial paper.

▲ **LESLEY TAYLOR**
Fly Stitch Laminate
A line of fly stitch (done
on silk) is laminated
between a base sheet of
cotton linters, with a
second sheet, made from
tissue paper pulp, on top.

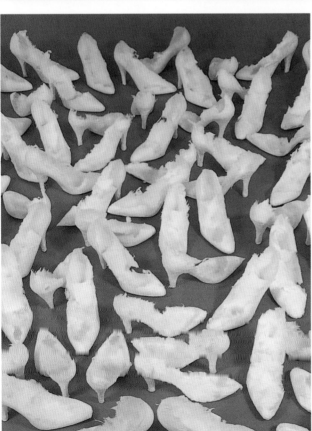

◀ **JANE PRICE**
Cast Paper and Human
Hand Holding Fig
Water iris and abaca pulp is
used to make the sheets
used in the casting of this
piece. The hand is poised to
pop the fig into the
waiting mouth, capturing
a moment in time.

◀ **SUSAN CUTTS**
Juliette
The artist's own handmade
paper from abaca pulp, in wet
sheet form, is used in the casting
of 500 pairs of paper shoes for this
installation. No glue or armatures
were used in the process.

Bookbinding Gallery

Bookbinding is an even older craft than printing. It wasn't long before the functional aspect—the recording and preserving of information—led to the perfection of technique and the development of bookbinding as an art form. Early bookbinders devoted their lives to the mastery of their craft, so that their books became examples of flawless craftsmanship.

Today, there are some who, with similar devotion and commitment, continue to use traditional forms and techniques. Others experiment with design and methods that allow for creativity and self-expression.

The books in this gallery reveal some of the innovative approaches to bookbinding as well as traditional styles with contemporary flair. Paul Johnson's "Flying House" pop-up features bold color in the intricate and yet wildly flamboyant book design. In Philip Smith's binding of *A Fine Balance* by Rohinton Mistry, each decision regarding materials, design, and embellishment has been made with regard to the content of the story within. Lois Polansky makes use of papercasting on the covers of her books in "Fantasy Masks and Other Body Parts." Enjoy this gallery tour. Let it stimulate your imagination and open up a world of possibilities to you as a bookbinder.

▲ **LOIS POLANSKY**
Fantasy Masks and Other Body Parts
The artist has used handmade cotton fiber cast in plaster molds for the unique covers of this book, with accordion-sewn pages and four mask paintings done with powdered pigment/encaustic. The folded book measures 14 x 10 x 6 in (34 x 25 x 15 cm).

▶ **LESLEY TAYLOR**
Banff Book
This is Book Two of a limited edition of ten handmade books using handmade paper. The pulp is made from scrap paper, the cover pages are poured and a small handwoven section is embedded in the front cover. A shell on the end of a linen thread forms the closure for this little book.

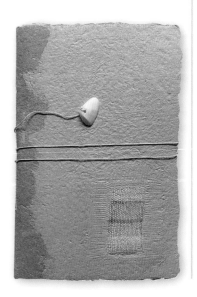

◀ **TONI SMITH**
Bark Book
The artist uses tree bark and Hawaiian lily paper. The pages have leaves and butterfly wings glued on and the binding is a stick attached with gold thread.

▼ **JOANNA POEHLMANN**
Bacon, Lettuce, and Tomato
Drawings in graphite and watercolor grace the pages of this collage accordion book. Ribbon ties are used for closure.

▼ **LORNA LEEDY**
Collecting America
Collectable stamps and drawing paper were used as a base for this accordion book with its own book box.

◄ ▲ PAUL JOHNSON
Flying House
The house's interiors (chairs, tables, beds) were constructed first, and the completed house exterior dropped over the rooms. The interiors were then dextrously glued together through the windows and doors. The wings were largely an improvisation.

◄ PAUL JOHNSON
Book of Hours
Watercolor paper and reactive dyes were used in making this exuberant pop-up book.

The constructions comprise fifty or more paper units that create myriad layered levels of design. The artefacts themselves combine the two cultures of aesthetics and science – one has to be an engineer to make the whole creative idea come into being. Architectural concepts are the foundation of my work, although thematic ideas derive from natural forms, landscape and religious iconography.

Paul Johnson

▼ NATALIE D'ARBELOFF
Pater Noster

This artist's book is one of an edition of five similar but not identical copies. Paper, fabric, and acrylics are all employed in the formation of the book which uses blind embossings with a concertina bound "stairway" construction. This means that the pages increase in size, forming a stairway when pulled out. The fabric-covered boards are painted with acrylics and embellished with felt and embroidery. The book is wrapped in painted cotton, tied with colored cords and held in a see-through pouch.

▲ CAS HOLMES
Blue Frog Book

The artist used an old photo album to create this book in which she has gathered memorabilia relating to her grandmother. Measuring 5½ x 3½ x 2 in (14 x 9 x 5 cm), the book is constructed using a method of layering and gluing.

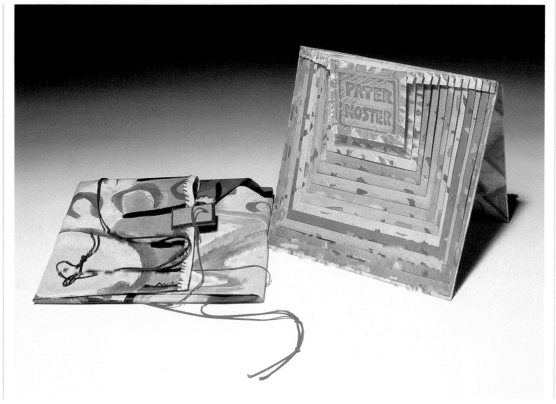

CAS HOLMES ▶
Bookleaves
Layered paper and leaves make up this 24–28 page book with a concertina style binding.

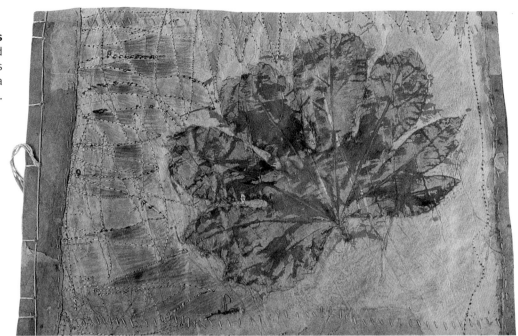

▼ GAIL STIFFE
VBG Occasional Publication II
The cover, made from recycled archival paper, encloses a commercial text block. Danish Millimetre binding technique is tied onto a cast paper cover.

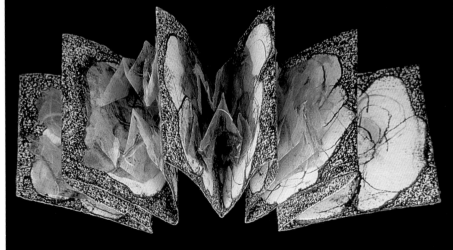

▲ SHEILA BENEDIS
Flower Book
Mixed media on paper. This handmade accordion book has folded inserts as well as handmade book pages.

▼ **LORI SAUER**
Complete Nonsense
by Edward Lear
This book is covered in
goatskin using a conventional
fine binding structure with
inlaid bands of leather and
onlaid black lines.

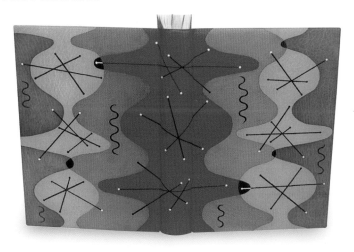

▶ **LIZANNE VAN ESSEN**
Planets
The artist has used handprinted
paper and card backing for this
accordion-fold pop-up book. She
comments, "My sculptural books
evolved from a delight in pure
form, with the play of light
creating shadows and volume.
I was excited by the
combination of
detail and strength,
and of simplicity
and complexity—
also by the surprise
element created
when the flat book
covers opened to
reveal thrusting
sculptural forms."

▲ **TONI SMITH**
Books A and B
Plant fiber and Tallowood leaves form
the base pulp for these books. Book A
is bound with a piano hinge. Book B
uses an exposed stitched binding.
Wallaby grass paper is used to cover
the books. The pages are recycled
mountboard in combination with
the plant fibers.

◄ **CAS HOLMES**
Slate-Leaf-Book
Cas Holmes has developed a technique of layering and laminating different papers to create a luminous surface. Using a collection of found papers, potato sacks, and conservation papers, the artist explores a book form using paper folding and covers the finished work in triangles of slate.

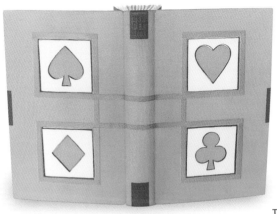

◀ **LORI SAUER**
Alice's Adventures in Wonderland and *Through the Looking Glass* **by Lewis Carroll**
These two books are bound together in goatskin using a fine conventional binding structure and decorated with rotating white panels each with a rotating inner symbol.

▼ **GAIL STIFFE**
Memory
This millennium book contains one page per decade. The plant fiber paper is made into sewn pages printed on an ink jet printer with the exception of the stenciled title page.

▲ **PHILIP SMITH**
Book Edge Painting
A commercial paper edition of *A Fine Balance* bound with exposed (painted) sections and yokes with title. The maril onlays continue in acrylic paint across the edges. This edition won the Booker Prize in Presentation Binding for 1996.

Glossary

Abaca
A plant, also called manila hemp, abaca (*Musa textilis*) is a relative of the banana plant whose long leaf-stem fibers are used in papermaking pulp.

Archival
When used to describe papers or boards, this term indicates that the material remains chemically stable over time.

Awl
A pointed metal implement with wooden handles, used for making preparatory holes in layers of paper, card stock, or cardboard.

Beating
The process of macerating plant fibers in order to break them down into pulp for the purpose of sheet formation. This may be done mechanically or by hand.

Bleeding
The spreading out of ink or paint on paper which has not been sized.

Boards
Hard covers, covered with paper or cloth, to create the solid front and back covers of a book.

Bone folder
A bookbinding tool used to press sharp creases without stretching or damaging the paper.

Bonding
The interaction between cellulose fibers and water which, when beaten and dried, adhere to form paper.

Brayer
A printer's hand-inking roller.

Casting
The process of making three-dimensional forms by pressing wet pulp into a mold.

Cellulose
The substance in plant material which enables the bonding of fiber to water to form paper.

Cooking
The process of heating plant fibers with an alkaline substance to break down the material and separate the usable from the unusable parts.

Cotton linters
Pulp produced from the fibers of the cotton plant and used in western papermaking.

Couching
The process of transferring a newly formed sheet of paper onto a prepared bed of woven material so that the water can be pressed out.

Deckle
The removable frame which rests on top of the mold to hold the pulp and define the edge of the sheet.

Deckle edge
The uneven, feathery edge created by the deckle, which distinguishes a sheet of handmade paper.

Duct tape
A wide, silvery, cloth adhesive tape.

Dyes
Soluble coloring agents that penetrate the actual structure of a fiber, and cling to it.

Embedding
Incorporating a decorative element into the sheet of paper during sheet formation.

Embossing
Forming indentations in wet paper by pressing a three-dimensional shape or texture into the fibers.

Exposed flute
Refers to the wavy pattern in corrugated cardboard. Usually sandwiched between two boards and hidden from view, craft stores sell exposed-flute cardboard, where the flute is visible.

Felt
The woven blanket used as a surface for transferring the newly formed sheet from the mold to the couching pad.

Fiber
The fine, threadlike filaments in plant tissue used to make pulp for papermaking.

Flax
A bast fiber from the blue-flowered plant *Linum usitatissimum*, from which linen cloth is made.

Flyleaves
The set of sheets, plain or decorated, placed next to the endpapers for protecting the book.

Fold and dip
The art of folding a piece of paper into a small rectangle or triangle and dipping the corners into dye.

Glue
Pliable adhesives used on the backs of many bindings; these are archival and easily removed.

Hemp
A bast fiber plant (*Cannabis sativa*) of high cellulose content. The fiber extracted from the stem is used to make rope and tough fabrics.

Hollander
A machine developed in seventeenth-century Holland, which turns raw fiber into pulp for papermaking.

Laminating
The process of layering together two or more sheets of newly formed paper to create a single sheet.

Maceration
The process of pulling plant fibers apart to make pulp.

Marbling
Creating decorative papers with a marble-like pattern by floating color on a surface and transferring the pattern onto paper.

Mitering
The process of finishing the corners of a book.

Mold
The basic tool of hand papermaking. A rectangular wooden frame, covered with a sieve-like laid or woven wire surface, used for sheet-forming in papermaking.

Papier mâché
The French for "chewed paper." A material made of pulped paper mixed with glue that can be molded when moist, and then baked to produce a strong but light substance that can be painted and polished.

Papyrus
An early form of writing surface formed from layers of the stalk of the papyrus plant (*Cyperus papyrus*), pounded into a sheet.

Parchment
A writing surface made from the skin of sheep or goats.

Paste
Adhesives made from wheat or rice flour, used to stick leather to spines, paper to paper, and paper to boards.

Pigment
Finely ground particles of color that require a retention agent to attach them to the fiber.

Post
The stack of newly formed sheets and couching material, before pressing.

Press
The device that exerts pressure on a stack of newly formed sheets to remove water and aid the bonding process.

Pulp
The general term used to describe prepared plant fiber or recycled paper combined in water to form sheets of paper.

Raffia
The fiber from the leaves of the Madagascar palm tree (*Raphia ruffia*).

Scoring
The practice of lightly marking paper with an incised line to make a sharp fold.

Sizing
The process of adding a starch or gelatin solution (a "size") to pulp or paper to decrease the paper's absorbency.

Tea paper
Paper made from papermaking fiber to which tea leaves have been added.

Vat
A rustproof container in which the pulp is combined with water and from which the sheets are pulled.

Vellum
A writing surface derived from the skin of stillborn or newborn calves or lambs.

White glue
A pliable, plastic based adhesive; it is non-archival.

Further Reading

PAPERMAKING

Dawson, Sophie, *The Art and Craft of Papermaking*,
Running Press, Pennsylvania, 1992.

Heller, Jules, *Papermaking*
Watson-Guptill Publications, New York, 1997.

Plowman, John, *The Craft of Handmade Paper*
Booksales, New York, 1999.

Reimer, Mary and Reimer-Epp, Heidi, *300 Papermaking Recipes*
Martingale, Washington, 2000.

Shannon, Faith, *The Art and Craft of Paper*
Chronicle Books, San Francisco, 1994.

Thackeray, Beata, *Paper – Making, Decorating and Designing*
Conran Octopus Limited, London, 1998.

Zmolek Smith, Gloria, *Teaching Hand Papermaking - A Classroom Guide*
Zpaperpress, Cedar Rapids, Iowa, 1995.

BOOKBINDING

Johnson, Pauline, *Creative Bookbinding*
University of Washington Press, Seattle, 1964.

LaPlantz, Shereen, *Cover to Cover*
Lark Books, Asheville, North Carolina, 1995.

Smith, Keith A., *Volume 1 Non-Adhesive Binding*
Keith Smith Books, Rochester, New York, 1997.

Thomas, Jane and Jackson, Paul, *On Paper: New Paper Art*
Crafts Council Gallery, London, 2001.

Suppliers

Suppliers of Papermaking
and Bookbinding materials

NORTH AMERICA

Botanical PaperWorks Inc.
329 Cumberland Avenue
Winnipeg,
MB R3B 1T2
Canada
tel: (204) 956-7393
toll free number:
(877) 956-7393
fax: (204) 956-5397
www.botanicalpaperworks.com

Handmade paper and
papermaking supplies, ribbons,
wax seals, vellum envelopes

Carriage House Paper
79 Guernsey Street
Brooklyn
NY 11222
USA
tel: (718) 599-PULP
fax: (718) 599-7857
orders: (800) 669-8781

Papermaking supplies

Lee Scott McDonald
PO Box 264
Charlestown
MA 02129
USA
tel: (617) 242-2505
fax: (617) 242-8825

**Twinrocker Papermaking
Supplies**
PO Box 413
Brookston
IN 47923
USA
tel: (765) 563-3119
orders: (800) 757-TWIN-8946
www.twinrocker.com

Cotton Press
1449 N. Angel Street Suite 1
Layton, Utah 84041
USA
tel: (801) 497-9298
fax: (801) 497-9308
www.cottonpress.com

Ceramic molds for
papercasting

Colophon Book Arts Supply
3611 Ryan Street S.E.
Lacey, WA 98503
USA
tel: (360) 459-2940
fax: (360) 459-2945
www.thegrid.net/colophon

Bookbinding and marbling
supplies

Cover Material Sales, Inc.
47 Warehouse Road
PO Box 566
Hyannis
MA 02601
USA
tel: (800) 225-7132
fax: (508) 790-2739

John Neal, Bookseller
PO Box 9986
Greensboro, NC 27429
USA
Tel: (800) 369-9598
Fax: (336) 272-9015
www.johnnealbooks.com

Talas
568, Broadway
New York,
NY 10012
USA
tel: (212) 219-0770
fax: (212) 219-0735
www.talas-nyc.com

CraftCo Industries, Inc.
410 Wentworth Street North
Hamilton, Ontario
L8L 5W3
Canada
www.craftco.com

Hobby Lobby
7707 SW 44th Street
Oklahoma City, OK 73179
USA
tel: (405) 745-1100
www.hobbylobby.com

The Papertrail
170 University Ave West
Suite 12–214
Waterloo, ON
N2L 3E9
tel: (519) 884-7123
fax: (519) 884-9655

UNITED KINGDOM

Two Rivers Paper Company
Pitt Mill, Roadwater
Watchet
Somerset
TA23 1QS
tel: (01984) 640128

The Paper Shed
March House
Tollerton
York YO6 2EQ
tel: (01347) 838253
fax: (01347) 838096
www.papershed.com

Faulkiner Fine Papers Ltd
76 Southampton Row
London WC1B 4AR
tel: (020) 7831 1151
fax: (020) 7430 1248

Shepherds Bookbinders Ltd
76B Rochester Row
London SW1P 1JU
tel: (020) 7360 1184

J. Hewit & Sons, Ltd
Unit 28, Park Royal Metro
Centre
Britannia Way
London NW10 7PR
www.hewit.com

Suppliers of equipment, tools, and materials for all craft bookbinding requirements.

Have agents and distributors throughout the world, visit web site for details.

John Lewis plc
Oxford Street
London W1A 1EX
tel: (020) 7629 7711
fax: (020) 7514 5319
www.johnlewis.co.uk

Beads, fabric, lace, ribbons

AUSTRALIA

Spicers Paper
82–90 Belmore Road
Riverwood
NSW
tel: (02) 9534 5544

Papercrafts Mailbox
31 Garrett Street
Carrington
NSW 2294
tel: (02) 4969 2543
fax: (02) 4965 4726
e-mail: ianola@coscom.net
www.mailbox.safeshopper.com

Paperpoint Sydney
21 Worth Street
Chullora
NSW 2190
tel: (02) 9335 1460

Peninsula Plaza Arts Supplies
20 Bungan St
Mona Vale
NSW 2013
tel: (02) 9979 6559

Scarlet Ribbons Needlecraft
45 Kiwan Street
Floreat
Western Australia 6014
tel: (08) 9383 9073
fax: (08) 9383 9074

Samuel E. Dantonio
53A Johnson Street
Mascot
Sydney
NSW 2020
tel/fax: (02) 9693 2226
email:
eddiedantonio@hotmail.com

Index

Numbers in *italics* refer to captions